About the author

For the past thirty years, Graham Andrews has had an interest in radio. In that time, he has worked in community radio in Australia, writing material for broadcast and presenting programs. Graham is a freelance writer, writing tutor and scientific editor. He is the author of ten books.

By the same author

A Guide to Wrought Iron and Welding

Easy Guide to Writing Winning Essays

Easy Guide to Science and Technical Writing

Easy Guide to Creative Writing

In Your New Image

Island of the Barking Dog

Dad Kept Bees

Reach For the Sky

Practical Arc Welding

YOU'RE ON AIR

A Guide to Writing, Preparing and
Presenting Programs for Community Radio

Graham J Andrews

Flairnet

First published 1995 by Currency Press

This Edition Copyright © Graham J Andrews, 2013

ISBN: 978-0-9875092-7-7

Published by Flairnet
www.flairnet.com.au
Post Office Box 645
Narooma NSW 2546
Australia

National Library of Australia Cataloguing-in-Publication entry

Author: Andrews, Graham J. author.

Title: You're on air : a guide to writing, preparing and presenting

programs for community radio / Graham J Andrews.

ISBN: 9780987509277 (paperback)

Notes: Includes index.

Subjects: Radio authorship.

Radio programs.

Radio broadcasting.

Dewey Number: 791.443

Contact the Author:
Website: www.grahamandrews.com
Email: graham@grahamandrews.com

Preface

It has been nearly twenty years since I wrote the first edition of this book. In that time, a lot has changed in community radio, but a lot has remained the same.

Broadcast technology is so different to what was available in the early 90s. Back then, digital radio was just starting to emerge, but not so in Australia. Now many stations around the world are either broadcasting in digital radio, or they are at least running test broadcasts, with the intention of full-time digital broadcasting in the near future.

Back only twenty years, music was played on CDs that were becoming popular, but much was still played on cassette tapes as well as on LPs, those cumbersome disks that were subject to warping, scratching, crackling and collecting dust that gave anything but a clear reproduction of sound. But it was about all we had, so we accepted them. We won't accept music that is interspersed with scratches and crackles now, because we don't need to. Modern recording devices can give incredibly clear reproduction of sounds.

Back twenty years, many community radio stations in Australia relied at least on a small contribution from their sponsors to raise money to buy whatever equipment they could. Any money the stations could raise by means of open days and public demonstrations was used to just run the studio. Public demonstrations were an important means of recruiting new members, new presenters. Now, many government grants are available so stations can buy good quality broadcasting equipment, and in turn present programs of a much higher standard.

Over those years, mainstream radio has changed. We no longer get the variety of programs we did even then. Most commercial stations are limited in what they present. The programs presented by the national broadcaster have changed, sometimes in response to listener demands, and sometimes because of budgetary constraints. Radio dramas are no longer heard. Radio serials disappeared long ago.

Media studies at schools and at universities are now playing an important role in training and introducing students to radio. This has enabled the range of programs to be presented on community radio to change too.

But some things haven't changed, and probably won't change for a long time to come.

People work in community radio as unpaid volunteers. Many have gained valuable experience by their voluntary work, and have gone on to build worthwhile careers for themselves in other broadcasting fields, or as commentators.

By giving their time, they have entertained thousands of listeners. But at the same time, those listeners have benefited from the range and the depth and quality of programs presented by the volunteers.

Training of presenters and those involved in the day-to-day running of community radio stations has improved. The audiences now expect, indeed demand, a much higher standard of programming.

This book provides a great deal of helpful advice to those involved in community radio. It should be a benefit to those involved in presenting programs, and those involved in writing news bulletins, and in making station announcements, such as sponsorship announcements. It should also benefit those who want to update their radio skills, and to learn just how much more there is in radio, and what they can do on air. So whatever your level of skill, this book should be a useful tool for extending your expertise and presenting programs that are truly worth listening to.

Contents

Acknowledgements

I wish to express my sincere thanks for the help and contribution that I received in writing this book. Particular thanks must go to my wife Glenden for proofreading the manuscript and making a number of helpful suggestions that have been incorporated into the text. I would also like to express my appreciation to all those I have worked with in community radio who have made my time in broadcasting an enjoyable and rewarding experience.

Introduction

It seems that a lot of people at some time in their lives have wanted to work in radio. Now, with community broadcasting firmly established in Australia and around the world, aspirants can have their dreams easily fulfilled. Community radio really is for everyone. Age is no restriction. Many people become presenters after their retirement, others contribute to radio while they are still attending school.

This book concentrates on community radio, because that is where there are opportunities to be creative with radio. Most commercial stations, and state-run broadcasters do not present the range of programs they did in the 1950s and the 1960s. But community radio can fill that gap. Community radio can be the starting point for many careers in radio, and your involvement in your community radio can be viewed as just the starting point.

Radio can be fun and exciting. But, for those not properly prepared and trained for the tasks ahead of them, radio work can also be a daunting experience.

While many people would like to write for radio, they do not know how to go about developing their ideas, or, once basic ideas are written down, how to develop them into material suitable for radio. Consequently, most programs on community radio stations are music programs. The aim of this book is to show that there is much, much more to radio than being just another disc jockey.

What's radio all about then? It's about entertaining people. It's about educating them. It's about amusing them. It's a process of enriching the lives of others.

At the same time, it should be a process whereby you, the writer or presenter of programs on radio, are fulfilled by being creative, producing and presenting programs that are fresh and original.

Radio is a medium for the sense of hearing alone. Block out all other senses, and radio is still there in all its richness. Writing for radio demands special consideration — how to achieve that richness through the exclusive use of sound. Radio is demanding, and therein lies the challenge.

Radio is about doing something that enhances your enjoyment of the arts and entertainment. Radio is a way to expand talents which you may not have had the opportunity to use in the past. It may be that you see a gap in existing radio programming and feel that others could benefit from, or appreciate a new and hopefully exciting type of program. Here's your opportunity to do something about filling that gap and providing the audience with something they want to hear.

RADIO IS A UNIQUE MEDIUM
Unlike commercial radio, community radio does not have sponsors dictating program policy and content. It is for everyone — it is there for everyone to listen to, and for everyone to become involved in. Yes, everyone. And that's what makes community radio so exciting.

The open, egalitarian nature of community radio means that you can offer your listeners more than many larger stations with their narrow formats. You can expand the range of your programs to include music (by far the most popular program to present), new dramas and radio comedies, or poetry readings which are seldom heard. Then there are the more serious programs on community radio, such as documentaries and news. All, more carefully tailored to the local audience.

Listen to radio as much as you can — community radio, public broadcasting and commercial stations. Don't just treat the radio as a source of background noise. Listen to programs that you like and try to analyse what it is you like about each of them—their formats, the way they are presented, the use of humour. Also listen to programs that you don't like, and similarly try to identify what it is that turns you off.

Many community radio stations run training courses for people who want to get involved. Ring your local station to find out more and establish contact.

A training session will only be a starting point. It will get you started and teach you the basics—which knob on the console does what. But it won't necessarily teach you all there is to know about radio, or give you a picture of its full scope. Training courses are essential, yet limited. It is up to you to make the most of community radio—your station. Time spent learning what can be achieved through radio and what it can offer you, as well as the listeners, will be time spent in a useful, enjoyable and rewarding way.

Whatever area of community radio you eventually decide to specialise in, you must learn the art of writing for radio. And editing. Editing is the art of re-writing, or improving any written work that you intend to present. Radio is not about using a lot of words. Good radio means using only the right words, and the right amount of those words. Try to abandon the belief that every word you write or say on air is sacred—be prepared to sacrifice surplus words. Deleting words, particularly from your own material, is like working in an overgrown garden—remove the weeds so that you can see the remaining gems with full clarity.

So let's start by looking at what goes into a radio script and how to put a script together.

Chapter 1 Writing Your Script For Radio

Some people can speak fluently without the use of notes. They can launch forth, as they put their thoughts together, without 'uming' and 'ahing' and producing the other meaningless grunts and groans that pepper our everyday speech. If you can do this, then you may feel that it would be a waste of time to meticulously produce a script and read from it, word for word. However, if you are not one of that very rare and fortunate breed, you should — must — write down everything you intend to say when the microphone is open.

Your script will keep you on track throughout your program. It will ensure that you say only what you intend to say, and no more. It will ensure that you say everything clearly, without repeating yourself unnecessarily. It will ensure that each part of your program follows from the previous one as was intended. If you become tongue-tied and find yourself floundering for words, there's your next sentence, right in front of you, waiting to be read. A script will remove the tension many presenters encounter when the microphone is turned on and they are 'ON AIR'.

Even with a well-prepared script, you may make some mistakes that will bring smiles to your listeners' faces. But that is part of the fun of radio.

A prepared script should also ensure that your program runs to the correct length. If you forget a large chunk (perhaps through tension) you will end up having to play a lot of music at the end of your spoken segment just to fill in the allotted time. Your script will help you to keep all the points, or all the segments, of your program in the correct, logical, well-prepared and well-considered order.

WRITING STYLE

A radio script should be close to conversational speech in style. Write in a personal, friendly way. This does not mean that 'ya write any ol' thin' and 'ope she'll do, will ya?' By 'conversational' writing, I mean a more informal type of writing than you could expect to find in a well-written book, or a journal or magazine that's been well edited. In writing for radio, you'll round out the 'they will' to 'they'll'; the 'who will' to 'who'll' and so on. In other words, write it just as you would speak it.

With radio, you can get away with breaking some rules of the English language—but avoid sloppiness. While many a successful radio script would probably be rejected if sent to a magazine for publication, because of 'poor grammar', be very careful not to take it too far.

One point in your favour is that, although some colloquial expressions look terrible on paper, at least no one other than yourself will ever see what you've written. Just ... be yourself: but, don't overdo it, or else no one will understand what you mean. The entire script must make sense—not only to you but, more importantly, to your listener.

The idea in radio is to create pictures and to stimulate the imagination of the listener, and this is achieved by the careful selection of words, not by the unlimited use of adjectives.

Every word must be the right word. Every word you use must have the precise meaning that you intend. Every adjective should fit the noun perfectly. Unintentionally humorous phrases will arise for as long as people continue to write or speak.

Make sure that the words you use are real words—don't make them up. The number of runs required by a cricket team are attainable—they are not 'gettable'.

Above all, for anything other than a news bulletin where the writing should be more formal—be yourself.

Avoid using clichés. Clichés are those tired, worn-out phrases, such as 'on the back burner', or 'level playing field', that seem to be used in almost every news broadcast. Frequent use has rendered such phrases meaningless. Don't use them. Their use creates an impression of a stale imagination and an inability to think in an original way. Think of new terms, new ways of expressing ideas. Be fresh – don't copy someone else's worn-out language.

Some words, or combinations of words, are very awkward to say. When writing for radio: if you can't say it aloud easily the first time, say it in a different way.

CHOOSING YOUR WORDS CAREFULLY

Before considering how you will say something, you must of course decide exactly what it is you are going to say.

The first rule of scriptwriting is: keep to the point! If it's not relevant, cut it out. You can always file away those less than relevant literary gems for another day, and another program, when they might fit better.

Decide what you want to say. Define the point you want to get across to your listeners. Then decide how you are going to say it – that is, in which order you will assemble all the information you want to convey. What is your listener interested in? What do they want to learn from your program?

Keep your language simple. Don't use complicated sentence structures that might confuse the listener – no long, seemingly endless paragraphs. Keep sentences short and snappy. Keep paragraphs concise and crisp. Always keep meanings clear. Remember your listener. If what you have written is too complicated to understand without hearing it repeated several times, it will be lost on the listener, who does not have the luxury of your script to go back to and re-read. If your listener has to spend time thinking about a sentence, he or she will probably miss the next three or four. You can regard that person as a listener that you have just lost—radios are very simple devices to switch off.

Like some magazine articles, radio talks can sometimes take a long time to get to the heart of what they are trying to say. Despite the fact that the subject matter might be very interesting, impact is lost if an article is too waffly and too wordy. The facts end up lost amongst the words. Be precise: your listeners will appreciate it and they'll want more of your programs.

Your first sentence should open the central theme of the program. Your second sentence should carry on with the story you are telling. The next paragraph should contain only information that follows on from the previous one. It should not contain a single word that isn't absolutely necessary to the story.

Ask someone to check the copy you prepare. When you read your own work, you will tend to read what you intended to write, rather than the words that are in front of you.

It's not just the words that make a sentence correct. Punctuation is as important as the words. An incorrectly placed comma can throw out the whole meaning of a sentence. An unnecessary pause, or a pause in the wrong place can make your words mean something quite different from what was intended.

THE AUDIENCE—YOUR LISTENER

I have been referring to 'your listener'. Although broadcasting can reach many people, radio is not about talking to the masses. It is about talking to your listener—one person. You may be talking to an audience of thousands, but you should treat each of your listeners as individuals, so write for one person, one listener. Radio isn't like television where several people watch a program in a room together. It's more personal. Many people enjoy listening to their radios for company as well as for entertainment, interest and enjoyment—the radio is often their friend too.

Just as you would be sincere when you talk to a friend, be sincere when you talk to your listener. If you have something to say, sound as if you mean it. There's nothing worse than listening to someone who sounds as if what they're reading is the last thing they want to say.

Always keep your listener in mind as you prepare a program. Identify someone who is typical of your audience. Then write as if you were talking to that person.

Your aim is to write your script so that the person you have identified can understand all of what you are saying. Ask yourself: 'Would Joe understand this?' If not, simplify the sentence or the paragraph. If you are giving practical instructions for a home improvement project, keep in your mind someone who could possibly be the world's most unhandy person. This will encourage you to write instructions that are precise and clear. Do not assume that your listener possesses any background knowledge that might be specialised. Yet be careful not to sound too patronising.

If you have any doubts about the general accessibility of your text, pick someone like yourself—a friend, perhaps, or a close relative—and see if they understand it. If they do, leave it; if they don't, fix it.

BUILDING YOUR SCRIPT—THE ART OF WRITING

It's about time we considered the art of writing for radio—that is, putting the words down on paper.

The first sentence is usually the hardest sentence of all to write. If you find yourself sitting and staring at a blank page or an empty screen for minutes on end with nothing happening, don't give up. Just ... write something. Get a sentence, any sentence, down on paper. Follow this with another sentence. If these first sentences seem like rubbish, remember, you can always discard them later. Often just the act of getting your first ideas down on paper will help other thoughts to flow. Edit them later—discard the junk but for now ... just begin.

Something that often prevents the first words from coming is the intimidating thought of the sheer volume of words that have to be written. For instance, a one-hour radio program might require around 10,000 words, which amounts to about forty pages of typescript. Do you believe yourself capable of writing this much material? Probably not; and your page will remain blank for a long, long time if you approach the task at hand in its entirety. The enormity of a task is often enough to detract any would-be author, builder, sculptor or scriptwriter from even beginning a project.

Your radio program will not be written all at once, but word by word, paragraph by paragraph, or page by page. Try to build up your story like a house — brick by brick, from the bottom up.

With a program requiring 10,000 words or more, don't think in terms of the finished piece, but in terms of the size of the units or bricks with which you feel most comfortable. This might mean a page, half a page, or a paragraph.

These small units, added one to the other, will soon become a full-length program — a few paragraphs, or a couple of hundred words a day will, in only a matter of weeks, add up to the 10,000 words you have to write. How long have you thought about starting that program you feel so strongly about? A year? More than that?

Seeing yourself making progress with your work as each 'unit' is written, can make the difference between the struggle and the triumph. If you get stuck with one section, don't stop, but work on another section that you feel more confident about. You will be in a better position to smooth any bumps and cracks when the larger part of the structure is in place.

Let's consider the hypothetical task of writing a one-hour program about, say, juvenile delinquency and suppose our own basic writing unit is two pages — that is, we know we can write two pages about almost anything. Our job is to break down the 10,000 words required into manageable writing units of two pages. But remember that a one-hour program (or, rather, a fifty-minute program that allows for station announcements, sponsorship messages and an introduction) won't consist of only the words you write. It will include interviews, other people's points of view, and, hopefully, much more. All these have to be taken into account.

The first step is a rough division that will form the main segments of your program. Let's say six segments, each one about fifteen hundred words, or six pages, long.

The first segment should outline your topic and define your terms. This in itself may seem intimidating, yet, broken down further, that first segment of the program becomes more manageable.

What is delinquency? My definition may possibly be different from yours, and different again from a social worker's … or, indeed, that of a high-court judge. So, perhaps ten definitions, each of a couple of paragraphs (adjusted to suit the script, of course) will take care of a major part of Segment One in your proposed program.

WRITING YOUR SCRIPT

Segment Two might consist of a number of paragraphs devoted to the types of minors who commit acts of delinquency. Difficult, but again, broken down into units, we may get ten different groups of people who become involved in anti-social behaviour — discuss these groups on the six pages allocated.

Segment Three might look at the socio-economic factors of known offenders (three or four paragraphs), educational background (a page), the psychological profiles of delinquency (one page), the background to some specific case histories, and family factors (each of a page or two).

Perhaps your units might be larger than two pages. That's great — try to compose a whole segment at a time.

Subsequent segments might look at cross-cultural differences: how is delinquency viewed in North America, in Australia or the islands of the Pacific?

As you write each segment you may well find that it is running too short or too long. Don't worry, the length of each section can be adjusted with editing.

Dividing a radio program into small writing units that you can concentrate on, one at a time, will also help to prevent it becoming boring, with plenty of action, description, ideas and opinions on every page. You will be able to create a story that will leave the listener unaware that you, the writer, struggled and sweated over each and every paragraph.

We all get annoyed with people who repeat themselves in conversation. But when you write for radio, a limited amount of repetition is alright. Often it is necessary to repeat a point, albeit in a slightly different way, just to make sure that your listener grasps what has been said, or to reinforce a point. With practice, you will soon develop an instinct for what needs to be repeated, and what's best not repeated. And, indeed, what's best left unsaid. Don't repeat whole paragraphs just to pad out a program so that it will fill the time allocated.

If you are writing drama for radio, employ the same technique of breaking the writing task down into small units before you begin to write. In drama, something should happen on every page: different incidents to involve your characters in, different people in different settings, different historical eras. Breaking down the task will help you keep the writing fresh and fast-paced.

It's your house you're building ... use 'bricks' that you can handle comfortably. Don't strain yourself handling bricks manufactured for someone else with capabilities that would outstrip even the most accomplished builder ... or writer.

PRESENTATION OF YOUR SCRIPT

Try to avoid page breaks in the middle of sentences. Similarly, avoid carrying one or two lines from the end of a paragraph over to the next page — there could be a pause, or a rustling of paper as pages are turned and the sentence is picked up.

The presentation of your script is important. Make sure that you use a good, dark ink in your printer. Use double spacing between lines — double-spaced scripts are much easier to read from. Select bond paper that doesn't crinkle loudly as the pages are turned — microphones are very sensitive these days.

LENGTH

How long should your script be? It's not so much a matter of how many pages, but more importantly how much time you have in which to get your points across.

As a rough guide, the average speaking rate is about 150–180 words per minute. So if you have one minute to make your point, you'd better write about two-thirds of a double-spaced page. A ten-minute talk will require about 1500 to 1800 words. Be aware: radio consumes an awful lot of words!

When you've written your script, edited it, and made sure it reads aloud alright, time a reading of it. If you intend reading it yourself, time yourself. If you are asking someone else to read it, time that person reading it. The average speaking rate quoted above should only be viewed as a rough guide. We all read at quite different speeds. Don't think it looks 'about right ... near enough'. It may end up running ten seconds over, or a minute under the allotted time. And that's bad radio production.

Finally, your script is ready for reading on air. It's probably best, if you're a good reader, to present it yourself. If your reading really isn't good enough, do your listeners a favour and get a fluent reader with a good radio voice to read it for you.

CONSIDER THESE HANDY HINTS

So you won't stumble when quoting dates, write them in your script as they are spoken, not as they would appear in print. For example, the New Year begins on January the first, not January 1. The financial year ends on the thirtieth of June, not June 30.

Take care with the use of adjectives. Make sure they mean something if you really have to use them.

Writing good radio material is like good writing for another medium — it should be a mixture of long and short sentences. Paragraphs too should be varied in length to lend rhythm and colour to your prose.

Check all figures, dates and weights. Units of distances can easily be misinterpreted.

CONSIDER THESE POINTS

Let's look at a talk that was prepared for radio, and see if it works according to the points considered in this chapter. Refer to the script reproduced in Appendix form at the back of the book (page 139). It is a script about declining soil nutrients and its bearing on soil quality. The script is of a type that could be used in a nature program or one on the environment. It contains nearly 2300 words, and would run to a fraction under fifteen minutes. The timing is critical, and planned, as this allows for a short introduction of about ten or twelve seconds, and about eight or ten seconds at the end of the program for the presenter to recap the title of the piece and the author's name. Read the script through a couple of times, taking notes if you feel inclined.

Ask yourself, 'Does this script work?' Consider the following points.

- Is it appropriate for the program?

- Is the timing right? The timing is critical, and planned. The length should allow for a short introduction of about ten or twelve seconds, and about eight or ten seconds at the end of the program for the presenter to recap the title of the piece and the author's name.

- Has the writer decided what he wanted to say, and then said it precisely and succinctly?

- Does each point follow from the previous one in an orderly, logical manner?

- Would it interest a listener to an intended program?

- Are there any phrases or sentences that are likely to cause the reader to stumble?

- Is it in a 'conversational' style — flowing smoothly, and easy to follow and understand?

- Would this talk maintain a listener's interest for the whole of the talk?

- Are the sentences short, or of varying length?

- Are the paragraphs the right length?

- Is the talk personal enough for radio — that is, has the writer directed it at one reader — on a one-to-one basis?

- Is the writer reminding the listeners of the main points by the careful use of repetition?

- Have any unnecessary words been used to pad out the material?

Chapter 2 Gathering and Presenting News

Community radio can, and should, play an important role in its capacity to present interesting and relevant news.

It is unlikely that any community radio station will have the technical resources available to larger, national networks, nor is it likely to have the budget to provide a comprehensive news service. However, the role that community radio can perform well is that of presenting local news — that is, news that is truly relevant to listeners within its broadcast range.

News need not necessarily be restricted merely to the events of the day. If a community radio station is dedicated to, say, the arts, the news can be predominantly about the arts. Or if a bulletin is scheduled for the beginning of a science program, then this could well be a short 'science news' segment that looks at new developments that have just been announced in the field of science.

But what is news?

The Macquarie Dictionary defines news as 'a report of any recent event or situation'. It goes on to add that news is 'information, events etc. considered as suitable for reporting; information not previously known.' The last part of this definition of news would rule out much of what is broadcast by some national stations! Questions also arise as to whether much that is included in those broadcasts comes under the category of 'suitable for reporting'.

News must be of interest and must be relevant to the listening audience.

The type of overseas news presented on most of the large networks is generally not that relevant to local communities — try to concentrate on events happening close to home.

Sift out news items that are not relevant to your particular radio station merely by asking yourself if an event is of direct and immediate interest to local listeners. If the answer is 'yes', then consider it for inclusion in your broadcast. Consider it at this stage, but don't necessarily pass it until you have looked at a few other points.

GOOD NEWS—BAD NEWS

There has been, for a long time, a saying that good news doesn't sell newspapers. This may be true, but does it also mean that all news should be bad news, full of gloom, despondency, abounding with hopelessness?

On most days, activities and events of many types happen in any community, large or small. There will be accidents of course. Perhaps a well-known family will lose its house in a tragic fire, perhaps a light aircraft will crash. More positive events will take place too. A large community effort could have raised enough money to enable a family that lost its home in a fire to rebuild their lives. A story like this will be cheering, despite its earlier 'bad news' aspects. Perhaps a local high school student might have come top of the State in the examinations. Or perhaps the town was judged as the tidiest of the tidy towns for the year.

Anyone gathering news could find all sorts of things that are not only 'good news' stories, but also well worth reporting. As a news gatherer, you have the opportunity to change perceptions in your locality in a positive way. Vary the content of your news broadcast. Be inventive.

LOPSIDED ADJECTIVES

Watch out for biased and dramatic use of adjectives. Unemployment, for example, can 'soar' if it increases by 0.1

percent during a month, but rather than 'plummeting' the same 0.1 percent the following month when the figures for unemployment are released, tends to 'creep slowly back'. Use only the adjectives that really apply to a term you are reporting on — if you need to use adjectives at all.

Don't add your own meaning to words unless those meanings actually apply. You can distort the news, either deliberately or unintentionally, if you do. Let the listeners make up their own minds about what is going on. Report the facts — don't impose your own prejudices upon the story.

Make each news story clear from the start. A listener does not have the benefit of time to consider what is being said and to go back over facts. News should be presented clearly and succinctly at all times. Be prepared to shorten items whenever you can, but in doing so make sure that you do not distort the meaning of the story you are condensing.

TIMING AND DEPTH

Just about any news item can be inadvertently stretched out to an unreasonably long and boring length. The fact that you feel passionately about a subject doesn't mean that your listeners give the subject the same priority. Never forget your listeners!

If too short a time is allocated to each item, perhaps in an attempt to include as many news items as possible, important details will be lost. Some stories do not require much time to report; others, because of their complexity, may need a lot longer. As a general rule, allocate enough time to each item of news to tell the story, and no more. Not even a second more! Most items of news can, and should, be reported in about twenty seconds — that is, about sixty words.

Once you have reported an event, move on to the next story. Avoid unnecessary detail. We all tend to view things as possessing different values. What is important or interesting to one person may not deserve any air time at all in the opinion of another person.

If you are personally involved with a group, organisation or particular event, you may be inclined to give that event far more time and reporting depth than another, perhaps equally worthy, event. So, if you are enthusiastic about an event, don't kill the story by over-reporting it. Keep your news items short and interesting and they will live long in the listeners' minds.

If you succeed in arousing your listeners' interest in a story, it is a pity not to follow that story through to its resolution. Telling your audience that Mr So-and-so hopes to achieve such-and-such next week will get the listeners interested; it would be a pity not to tell them next week that Mr So-and-so achieved what he set out to do, and went well beyond his aims. This type of story should be entered in a diary and followed up to its natural conclusion.

LENGTH

How long, overall, should your news bulletin be? A ten-minute news bulletin will require about 1500 words. Even a slow reader would easily get through 1500 words in ten minutes. If enough material has not been prepared, it is the reader, suddenly confronted with the shortfall in material, who will have to fill in the remainder of the time.

Less may well end up being more. The length of each item of news is critical — to maintain interest, and so that only the main facts are reported. This is where good radio writing skills and editing skills are essential. As mentioned above, twenty seconds broadcast time, or about 60 words, is adequate for most news items in a bulletin. An item of major significance could run a little longer — perhaps up to a minute — but it truly must be an important item for this extra time to be justified. If twenty seconds seems too long, there is nothing wrong with making some items of news run to only ten or fifteen seconds. A story's length is dictated by its importance and by the availability of other news. However, don't take this as a cue to pad out a minor item of news because nothing much happens on a particular day.

It would be better to find a few more items to include in the bulletin or, if you really can't track down any more items, lengthen some of the more important items by perhaps one sentence each.

LOBBYISTS, STATISTICS, BIAS AND FACTS

As a news gatherer, you will invariably find some organisations or individuals who want to be heard more than they think anyone else has a right to be heard. Be careful of these individuals or organisations. Such groups may be good for occasional copy, but hopefully your community consists of more than one interest group. Most people like some variety in their lives. Groups that tend to be vocal will often try to bluff their way into the news for every point they wish to make. Usually, though, you will find that what they want to say isn't really newsworthy to anyone except themselves.

It may be hard sometimes to distance yourself from some issues, particularly in a smaller community, but you must be unbiased in your reporting, regardless of how you feel about a subject. And don't think that leaving an item out of a bulletin because you can't be unbiased is going to help you – this is just as bad as writing the copy in a biased way. It may be hard, but you must succeed in this respect in every story you write.

For every organisation in your community that takes a stance, there will be another that adopts the opposite position! For those who wish to see smoking banned, there are other groups pushing for the freedom to smoke; abortionists often clash with anti-abortionists; those wanting an increase in the size of national parks will meet a group who want logging freed up; and if there are people who want to increase parking fees, others will freely admit that they believe all parking should be free, as a civic right!

Yes, indeed there are always different sides to every argument. You will realise this the first time you report one side of an argument and not the other. But this is not to say that the views of all opponents or proponents can, or should, be reported with the same vigour! If the shire president says, for example, that tourism has increased in the area and that he believes this will be good for the community, then it is not absolutely necessary to counter this with the viewpoint of someone who disagrees.

Learn who you can trust with news. Be careful, too, of statements that are given to you, or press releases that are sent to the station for inclusion in the news. Sometimes a simple check of figures or the facts will show how ridiculous some such statements — and contributors — can be.

A quick check will often show how ridiculous some information is. Check the figures in all press releases and discard those that plainly stretch the truth. And if you find an error or mistake, check the copy even more thoroughly. You will often find several more mistakes, or 'things that simply don't add up'. Develop a policy with other people's material that you edit — check everything extra carefully, even if you have to contact the author of the source material. Don't look ridiculous yourself — throw bad or misleading copy out. It has no place in a news broadcast.

NEWS GATHERING

Where do you find news? Some reporters would say, 'anywhere that one cares to look'. Others might say that there never is any news, even in a city full of interesting events involving diverse people, moods and actions.

Local news, such as that provided by community radio stations, should cover local issues. Generally, people obtain most of their information about overseas and national events from the evening television news. Community radio stations can supplement that information admirably, and should concentrate their efforts on doing this well.

Although lots may happen in a town or a city, you, the news gatherer, must decide whether your audience will be interested in a particular event. Decide if a lot of people know a particular person who has done a particular act or deed. Is a particular event significant to a large number of people in your listening range? If, for example, an old brickworks in town closed down after a hundred years of operation, many people could relate to those premises; if it had been operating for a year and was closing for a month due to poor demand for its products, then, perhaps, the event would not be as newsworthy. You, as news gatherer and, quite likely, editor too, must decide on what your listeners need to know.

Encourage other members of the station crew to keep you informed of newsworthy events. Through the diversity of their own contacts, you will often find you have a surprising number of 'reporters' giving you leads. Each person involved with the station will associate with different groups of people, make different acquaintances in their lives, and be a source of information when you need it. This shouldn't prevent you from building up your own contacts to call on regularly for information and leads. Again, find out who you can trust. Once you have formed a group of contacts in, say, the police or a government department, let them feel that they can trust you, and that you are reliable enough to report information that they give you accurately and without bias. Get to know councillors personally — they will often give you helpful information about what is happening in council, and may well provide you with the names of other useful people to contact. You may be encouraged to sit in on council meetings where important community decisions are made.

COMPILING YOUR BULLETIN

You may have spent time in the studio, or out and about, collecting recorded interviews; you may have been on the telephone checking facts and gathering items for a bulletin. Now you must compile your news bulletin. But what comes first?

The order in which items are presented is important: the leader, or first item, should be the most important item of the bulletin — it is the responsibility of the news gatherer and news editor to place items of news in order of priority. After the leader, items should follow in order of importance to the community.

When is news no longer news? Only continue a news item if it continues to develop, and know when to cut it out of a bulletin. News becomes stale very quickly. Once listeners have heard an item they certainly don't want to hear it again and again.

Try to maintain a healthy balance of news. Life is a mixture of many things, and this should be reflected in the diversity of the news that you compile. You can aid diversity by grouping similar items together, such as mentioning three strikes in the one item, or two controversial council decisions on development under a collective news item concerning council matters.

RECORDED MATERIAL

A popular way to make the news lively and interesting is to play recorded interviews that relate to a news item. These should be kept short and well edited. Interviews could be with witnesses, or participants in an event. Interviews add variety to the news and depth to the reporting by the inclusion of other 'points of view'. But there are potential traps to be avoided.

You may well have to edit recordings heavily to extract only parts that relate to the item being reported. Cut out any meaningless words from the recording, such as 'Well ...' All the 'ers' must be deleted. Very few people speak fluently into a microphone and say exactly what they want to say in ten seconds or less. You may have to be ruthless in your editing of the recorded material.

Ensure consistency of facts between any recorded material and the script that the newsreader must follow. For example, if an organiser says that there were 2000 people attending a charity concert, then the newsreader should refer to the same number of people. Consistency is not hard to achieve, but it is if carelessness is allowed to creep into the writing or editing of news bulletins.

Beware: some recorders don't always work when you want them to. As a precaution against mechanical and technical mishaps, include a summary of the recorded segments in the newsreader's script so that in an emergency the reader can say '... we can't present that interview with Mr Spoonbender, but he said that ...' An accurate transcript of taped material will also help the newsreader to follow the script and know when the interview is about to finish.

CONTINGENCY ITEMS

You may feel you have written enough material to accurately fill a ten-minute bulletin. However, people speak at different rates; individuals can vary in the speed at which they read aloud from day to day. To prevent the reader's embarrassment after nine minutes of a ten-minute bulletin when he or she finds there is no more material to read, include one or two short contingency items at the end of the bulletin script. They may not necessarily be needed, but don't feel you have wasted your time by including them — one day your extra effort will be appreciated.

The copy should be given to the reader with sufficient time for it to be read and digested, and to allow the reader to mark any emphasis they may need to make. Copy that you have written may be read with different emphasis by someone else.

HANDY HINTS

Here are some handy hints that will make a big difference to the way you write a news bulletin.

Make news bulletins concentrated, smooth, not too informal, and not too fast or slow. Don't overwhelm the listener with the facts. Keep it simple.

You may have material that can be used in another program as well as in the news bulletin you have compiled. Perhaps the item you are reporting is too long, or too involved for a news broadcast. Report the details if they warrant reporting on the news, then pass the rest of the copy, including recorded interviews if you have them, to another presenter who may be interested in using the material in a different program, such as an arts program.

Be careful with references to time. Always be aware of which bulletin you are compiling the news for. If you prepare the copy in the morning for broadcast in the afternoon, ensure references to time are relevant to the afternoon, not when it is being compiled.

If a place you need to mention is a long way from your audience, then tell your listeners roughly where the place is in relation to a well-known location. If you are in a town somewhere in Central Victoria, and you need to mention say, Exmouth, then say Exmouth, north of Perth in Western Australia. Many people have not travelled far, and lots of places are still unknown to them.

Chapter 3 The Radio Documentary

A radio documentary is more than a mere presentation of the facts. A documentary should be an in-depth examination and consideration of an issue from a number of angles, including interviews with, and debates between, people with opposing views of a central issue. All aspects should be considered in a well-developed, unbiased manner.

In radio documentaries, sounds and words are working together to create a picture for your listener, rather than describing something that is flat, and boring. If you stimulate your listener's imagination, imagine how much more enjoyment they will receive from your program. If you record sounds on a riverbank, or on the beach, and your interview is held in that location, then, to your listener, they will be there too! Words will be one thing, but the sounds that accompany those words will transform the scene from a studio to the great outdoors — or wherever the interview is taking place. And as radio is a medium for sound, then radio documentaries are one of the best ways to use sounds to create vivid pictures.

Local issues are important to local communities, although, of course, State or national issues may encroach on local issues. So, what would be a typical issue worth making a documentary about, and what should be left out?

A topic such as the renewal of fishing licences would be of little interest to people living in major cities where most of the major networks are based. As a result, discussion of such topics isn't often included by a national or State broadcaster. Yet at a local level, say in a coastal country town, people would welcome news and discussion about such a subject. Pursuing the idea further, these same people are probably not going to be interested in the planning of a bridge, hundreds of kilometres inland.

With the use of small and very portable recording devices, a producer is able to move around a lot and record sounds from all sorts of different locations. It is possible to talk to people in their own familiar surrounds, in which the producer can capture the activity and the feel of everyday life. Feelings, attitudes, opinions, their own personal stories, all told first hand, are what radio documentaries are all about.

All these rich sounds, which all have a place, provide realism that can activate the imagination of the listener, and make them feel part of the scene, or location. Through the recording of sounds, voices and scenes (created through words) listeners have access to people and events they would not otherwise be able to be part of.

Documentaries can cover any range of subjects — life histories, a career in film or television as seen through the experiences of one person or one film studio, the rise of a well-known business person, or the life of a bushranger who roamed the hills out to the west of town. Some suitable topics could include social issues, mental illness, prison reform, science, land degradation, the development of radio and book publishing. Documentaries produced for community radio may well evolve from some aspect of a story covered in a news bulletin.

After radio drama, documentaries perhaps provide the most demanding, interesting and exciting creative challenge to writers and producers working in radio. There are so many aspects of a single issue to consider — research that reveals new material, interviews with interesting people who knew someone important fifty years ago, perhaps someone who can reveal a lot about a town's present-day character, or its people. Then there's the writing to link together the various segments of the program to consider, the music to link or break segments, and the editing and rearranging of recorded material to produce a program that is worthwhile and satisfying to listen to.

The everyday world is a dynamic world, full of people who are individuals, who all have their own lives, their own stories to tell, they all have a range of feelings from anger, frustration, pity, grievance, sorrow and lots more.

In preparing a radio documentary, it is not your job to interfere with these emotions, thoughts and actions of the individual, but to explore them, explore their origins, and their likely outcomes. Capture them in your recordings, and share them with the world — or at least with other listeners.

Don't try to force your preconceived ideas on the public to gain their support. Such attempts usually result in the opposite effect. Present the facts as best you can, in the most effective way. You will of course get people who disagree with you, no matter what you say. You will get others who agree with you entirely. Often the documentary maker will be caught in the middle of both extremes of view.

A good documentary should never be low on substance, fact or issue. Above all, the issues should be intelligible to the listener, easy to grasp, and easy to appreciate. This is the role of a good writer and producer. If your documentary is wishy-washy, how is the listener going to appreciate the issues you raise?

THOROUGH RESEARCH

Your first job, even before you begin your documentary, will be to understand your chosen topic fully. Is the person you are making the documentary about really famous? How did they achieve success in their field? What led to those achievements? Is this fame real or imaginary? Is there really a crime wave in a particular district or is it merely made out to exist? What sorts of crime is the district experiencing? How long has it been going on? Is there an end in sight? What did the lone bushranger get up to? How did he achieve notoriety? Were his crimes serious compared to those encountered in modern society? Was he captured? His sentence? The impact of bushranging in the community in those days? Many areas will have a local historian who has gone out of their way to gather material on all sorts of topics. They would be well worth your time talking to.

Groundwork for a well-produced documentary will entail far more than checking out local news material. It may involve research in a library, old records, council records, materials held by historical societies. Published local histories can be an immensely useful source of reference material to get you started in the right direction for this type of program.

LENGTH AND STYLE

A twenty-five- to fifty-minute program would be a good length to aim for when compiling a documentary — that's enough time to present even the most complex of material in a very interesting and thorough manner. A good documentary should be long enough to tell the story — no more, and certainly no less. No waffly writing; no padding out. The writing of a documentary, like all other forms of writing, should be clear, concise and crisp. Say what you intend saying in one sentence, instead of one paragraph. Leave out every word that you can without jeopardising style and clarity.

Using the right words will help bring the subject of a documentary to life. Consider the life of a bushranger roaming over the hills, hiding in caves, travelling on horseback across rolling hills, stealing cattle and droving them through steep mountain passes, and much, much more. As with all good writing for radio, every word must be the right word, spoken clearly, communicating exactly what was intended.

The art of good radio documentary production is to produce it to make sure that each section flows smoothly into the next section without making it look contrived, or so the listener thinks there might be a bit missing from the program. Without the natural flow, the program could end up as a succession of narration and cuts thrown together. Although I mentioned the 'natural' flow, in reality the production will be anything but natural, with clips of recorded material from this interviewee, a sentence or two from that one, your own scripted paragraph. However, when your documentary is ready to go to air, that's when it should all sound so natural, uncluttered, unhurried, and smooth in its flow, with a logical progression.

A common mistake with amateur documentary producers is to use unnecessary words to describe a scene, or an event. If you use a familiar sound – a telephone ringing, or a cash register, don't tell your listeners that the telephone rang … sound of telephone ringing … The cashier rang up the purchase … sound of a cash register ringing … This type of scripting worked well in episodes of the BBC's production of The Goon Show in the 1950s, but this is now the twenty-first century!

Always remember, when making radio documentaries, that sound has its unique way of communication. It will communicate colour, and action, mood, behaviour, and more.

Sounds, when used appropriately, can draw your listeners into the scene, make them feel part of the scene, and even part of the action. They become an integral part of the unfolding story. Now isn't this more interesting than describing the scene in the first couple of minutes, and having the rest of the program devoted to your voice, and that of one or two others in the studio? I am sure it is!

MUSIC

While most types of music can be used with good effect in presenting programs, music used in radio documentaries, if used at all, should be specially chosen to illustrate a point or create special effects. For example, you might use verses of a ballad to illustrate some aspect of a bushranger's life story. Music that is directly applicable is alright to use; other music is not, and merely serves as a waste of the listener's time. If your documentary is about floods, then music or songs about heavy rain may be used for emphasis. Music is good for setting moods or hinting at emotional states.

RECORDED MATERIAL

Most documentaries will entail a lot of interview segments, but not necessarily one interview run for its entirety. Breaking up a long interview into a number of short segments can produce an interesting effect. Play a short segment of one interview, cut into that with another short interview, perhaps a few lines of the ballad, then play another segment of the first interview, and so on. This is achieved of course with editing, when all the material that you need has been collected and production can proceed. Compilation should only begin when all the material is at hand. Having ready access to all the relevant material makes your final job much easier.

With all recorded material, sound quality is of paramount importance — it must be top quality, even if the interviews are recorded in difficult situations. All dialogue should be clear.

In a well-produced documentary, the interviews, either on their own or accompanied by other interviews, should be presented with minimum narration. Your narration should be to simply bridge segments or introduce a new speaker. An introduction will of course be required, as well as a conclusion. Lengthy pieces of narration detract from the overall effectiveness of a program.

If, for example, you are interviewing a very old man, his old-sounding, quivering voice will add character to the program. No amount of good writing will compare with the resonance of such a voice.

With every story, there will always be two sides to it. One, the truth, the other, well, …

If you are interviewing, say, councillors about a controversial decision that was made many years earlier, or the planning procedure for a structure the council gave your town many years ago, then interviewing a councillor from that time will give you one view. Residents, of course, will see things differently, and will probably disagree with everything the councillor says. That's alright though, because you are balancing up the whole background of the issue.

History can always be viewed from many different angles, always resulting in a different view. So, in many ways, you will have to balance the program, and interview people from both sides of the debate. And, possibly, thirty years later, both sides will still be squabbling. The main things is, if you can, get first-hand accounts of the issue for your program, and use sound — in his case the human voice — to good effect.

In many documentaries you will produce for community radio, you must make yourself familiar with all issues of the debate before you start interviewing even the first person. It's alright to get a general background in a casual discussion before you start recording, but when you get down to the serious business of recording your segments, you should be familiar with all aspects of the issue, even if it relates to issues that occurred thirty or more years earlier. If you don't prepare yourself well beforehand, your program will be very shallow and not very interesting. And you don't want to produce a program of that standard!

When you ask a question of anyone, always make sure you ask only one question, and out of politeness, always wait for that person to answer. Never ask two or three questions in the one, because some people, especially older citizens, will often forgotten what the third part of the question was before they have answered the first part.

DOCUMENTARY PLANNING AND STRUCTURE
An easy mistake to make when planning a documentary, is to try to cover too broad a subject. If you were planning a program about a large and complex subject, say mental illness, you would be well advised to look at a particular aspect of the larger topic. There is the treatment for the mentally ill that could be

considered; mental hospitals and the services and facilities they provide; or changes in the care of the mentally ill over the past few decades. You might perhaps look into the incidence of certain types of mental illness, such as schizophrenia. Decide on the limits before you begin your research.

A WORKED EXAMPLE

Let's look at the treatment of schizophrenic patients as an example. Initially, ask yourself questions to define the subject and the debate. Listeners will want to know how such a patient might feel at different times, during different circumstances, during different parts of the day. Is the treatment given for this illness effective? Is it long-lasting? Is there new treatment possible in the foreseeable future? Are mental hospitals effective in the treatment of this condition? How do the sufferers cope with their relatives and friends? How do relatives and friends cope with them? How does it affect their relationships? Their work? Their interests and hobbies? Listeners would probably like to hear directly from schizophrenic patients, as well as from doctors who treat them, and social workers who work closely with the families and friends of these patients.

Decide who would be the best people to interview for each aspect of the story. There will be doctors: do you know a doctor who would be willing to talk about this subject? Could you interview specialists from a hospital? Why not try contacting a relevant organisation that handles matters such as schizophrenia or mental health issues? Let each person tell their story, to contribute what they can, and let the story unfold through them — through their voices.

Recorded voices should sound natural — not at all contrived. If an interviewee speaks with hesitation, then that is the way the person speaks, and there is nothing you can do about it. Naturally, if someone speaks too slowly, you would be wise to limit the length of the interview.

Background noise, unless it interferes with the intelligibility of an interview, will probably add atmosphere to a segment — the sounds of a hospital would be extremely difficult to simulate.

Ambient noise can add effect. Suppose, for example, you are interviewing a mentally ill patient who walks slowly, and you inadvertently record the interview while walking along a gravel pathway. The slow footsteps will need no further explanation and will add power and pathos to the interview.

You may be lucky and find that one interview ends on a point that leads into the beginning of the next interview that you intend using. No bridging material in the form of narration needs to be included when these points fall back to back — one interview is faded out, the next faded up. Perhaps the next interview might add to the points made by the previous person, or perhaps contradict them altogether.

SOUND EDITING AND PRODUCTION

Eventually you will have recorded all the interviews that you intended making, and you will have all the background material you could possibly need. What then?

You would most likely have recorded too much material, and that is often a good thing — you can be ruthless and dispense with the material you don't need, instead of believing that every recorded word is sacred and needs to be preserved or, worse still, used.

From all the material available, decide what is important to your story, and what isn't. If most of an interview is relevant, but one sentence is not, then begin by cutting out that one sentence. Then cut out what is not relevant or needed from the next interview, until most of the material that can be disposed of has been eliminated. Eliminate unnecessary pauses — the 'ers' and 'ums' that seem to be part of everyday speech. Unless repetition of a point is really desirable — perhaps for a particular effect — if more than one person makes the same point, then cut it out. This will make valuable air time available for more important statements.

To obtain the best order for the interviews and narration, you might find it helpful to write down a summary of each interview — the beginning, the end line, the subject and the interviewee. Also note down the length of each section — in minutes and seconds — so that you can keep track of how long your program will run. You will usually find that you have to cut back further at this point, to achieve the correct running time.

Variety is the spice ... and this is particularly true in radio. Vary the interviews. Have contrasting voices following one another. Intercut sentences of varying length, and interviews of varying length. If every interview were exactly two-and-a-half minutes, your documentary will soon become monotonous to listen to. Such stylistic considerations must obviously be secondary to the clarity and overall structure of the documentary.

THE CONCLUSION AND THE END

The ending of a program is the part that is going to leave the listener with something to remember. A particularly effective way to end is to have one interviewee making a final point that, in some way, sums up the whole subject of the documentary. End on that sentence. Don't linger on, drawing out the end. Don't slow down the pace and spoil an otherwise effective ending. Ending with recorded sound can leave a strong impression with the listener. Suppose you are concluding the documentary on the mentally ill: a recording of the background noise on a psychiatric ward might well be more effective than a sober, concluding voice. Who is likely to forget the scream of a patient?

A good documentary should not end when the program itself ends. Its effect should remain with the listener well after the program has finished. The ending can leave the listener to make up his or her own mind about the issue being dealt with — a poignant ending leaves questions in the air.

The Radio Documentary

So, go on. Be creative. Be imaginative. The world is yours, and the world is full of excellent material for a radio documentary.

I mentioned a few possible themes for radio documentaries at the beginning of this chapter. Here are just a few more you could consider. Consider them mainly from the point of view of topics, and the range of subjects that are available for a radio documentary.

What would have happened if certain key events in our history had never occurred. How would your home country now be if certain events had not occurred?

Every town, every village, has monuments, or plaques. If your even small town has a number of these, then the history and significance of these together could make interesting listening. Explore your region's fascination with monuments, memorials, plaques and statues.

Look at aspects of the life of Mary MacKillop — the Melbourne woman who co-founded the Sisters of Saint Joseph of the Sacred Heart and became Australia's first Saint on the 17th of October 2010.

A soldier's daughter or son visits the places where their father served during a recent skirmish overseas, and shares his last letters home and his love of life in the place he died.

For the small permanent population, life can be very demanding, particularly over the winter. But in the summer many areas, particularly along the coast, become increasingly popular holiday destinations. Look at how more property than ever is owned by people who don't live there. What are the consequences on house prices?

A young family leads a busy urban life and moves to a small country village. Describe his attempts to learn the art of living off the land — something many of us only dream of doing.

Look below the surface of the names of people we encounter every day to consider the lives, and the emotions, of the people in our society.

Visit some of your regional national parks, and talk to the visitors, and the park rangers there, and see what the parks are all about.

There's a food festival in your region. Explore tastes, and sounds of such a festival — making coffee, roasting nuts, cooking oysters.

What about a documentary covering the history of a most local and iconic band?

There are plans for the Eco Village Project. The hunt is on for a site in your region for an ecologically sustainable co-housing community. What's that all about?

Writers and thinkers can nominate the work they think has done the most to create your country, or your region, to develop a notion of who we are, and where we have come from. Have you every thought of these answers yourself? Probably your listeners haven't either!

HANDY HINTS

If you track down old archival material, such as old records from a library, you could use an actor to read the relevant material as part of the documentary — as if the person concerned were reading the words. This can add a lot of drama and colour to the subject.

Many things are better said by the interviewees themselves. Let them tell their own story.

The beginning of a documentary, the first sentence, must grab the listeners' attention. But the narrative of a documentary need not start off, say, when a bushranger first started on his career of crime. It could start with the drama of his last stand.

Don't preach to your listeners, or hector them. Let them draw their own conclusions, based on your artful presentation of facts.

Chapter 4 Writing Radio Drama

Radio drama enjoyed pre-eminent success and popularity until the 1950s and 1960s when television began to take over as the dominant form of home entertainment. As pictures entered the home for the first time, the superficially inferior medium of radio became marginalised. The fact that modern-day audiences cannot compare in size to those of the heyday of radio doesn't mean that radio drama isn't still popular, and that there isn't an important place for it, even now.

There are many people who still like to hear the occasional repeated episode of their favourite dramas. A lot of radio listeners grew up with radio dramas and serials, and have fond memories of such entertainment.

Radio drama will always have a niche. There will always be times when people want something more involved than the usual rotational play of music. There will always be circumstances when people listen to the radio, either through choice, or because at a particular time they are unable to watch television, for example while tinkering under the bonnet of a car. Radio, including radio drama, keeps motorists company as they drive along lonely highways. Radio drama is no more dead than radio itself! Both are very much alive, and will undoubtedly remain that way.

Some people may not regard the writing of a radio drama to be as glamorous as writing a script for a television audience — partly, perhaps, because of the lack of financial remuneration. But there are rewards to be had in radio drama that can be every bit as significant as those found in writing for any medium, great or small.

WRITING A RADIO DRAMA

In writing radio drama, a very particular approach must be taken to script construction and writing style. This is the distinctive challenge of the art. Like all radio material, radio drama involves the stimulation of the imagination, not the laborious construction of tangible images. With the right sound effects, it is possible to create any sort of illusion. Whatever kind of drama you produce, it must create an image for the listener. That's the only way to put the action in a setting. It's possible, like in cinema or television, to place the characters in paradise. With the right sound effects, the right choice of words, it's possible to transport those characters from paradise to a parched desert island. Add a few sharks for good measure, or a plague of flies. A few appropriate sounds, acting to fit the part, the right dialogue, and there they are, as far as they could be from their paradise.

Many stage producers, actors and writers find that they can express themselves through the arts in a way that they would not otherwise be able to do. Through a performance that has a message, or acting that is convincing, they are able to express their attitudes, beliefs and emotions. Radio drama can have the same benefits. There can be a real message.

Some people express their emotions through anger. Radio can provide an excellent and constructive way to express how and what you feel, how you feel about the government or your workplace conditions.

The dramatic form does not allow for the lengthy scene-setting descriptions or illuminating inner thoughts that often form the backbone of the short story or the novel. Information has to be conveyed through dialogue – and it must not be blatantly obvious that the speaker is simply telling us (the audience) scene setting information that the writer needs to get across.

It would sound ridiculous if a character said: 'I like that blue and white dress you are wearing. You must have paid twenty-five dollars for it.' Instead, we could have a character say something like: 'Same dress? I might have known.' The reply could impart the information about the price of the clothing, and at the same time hint at the wearer's financial situation: 'I only had twenty-five dollars to spend. It's all I could afford. You never give me any more money to spend on myself.'

It's not what is said that is important, but rather how the information is conveyed to the listener to create a certain image. With radio, it is important at all times to get the listener to build up a picture in his or her mind of what's going on, who's wearing what, the actions of the characters, and what's happening outside, or even elsewhere in the room.

It would not be realistic to have one character say to another, 'There's John, who was sitting in the corner on the chair. I am angry that he has just got up' and expect listeners to get excited! Instead, information such as this can be conveyed by another character, say his father, shouting at John: 'Sit in that corner like I told you to, and don't you move again!' We now know that John is no longer sitting in the comer, he had been told to do so, and we know that the father is angry. You have to work hard to stimulate another person's imagination, but it can be done, simply with words — the right words, at the right time, phrased in the right way.

Although the text is the starting point of drama, the tone, or the way the actors say those words is important too. 'Sit in that corner like I told you to, and don't you move again', could be said brusquely, in a kindly manner, or in a nasty, spiteful way. The tone will reflect the type of character saying those words and that character's present mood.

DRAMATIC TENSION

The two mainstays of radio drama are the characters and the conflict. If one aspect is weak, the whole dramatic structure will collapse. Remove the characters, and naturally there's no one present to carry the conflict or action. Remove the conflict, and the characters remain quite normal, well-behaved, placid people.

To put it another way, if we removed all the conflict from our everyday lives there wouldn't be much to talk about, would there?

Conflict is caused by all sorts of circumstances arising from everyday situations. It's often caused by reaction. Conflict is personal—it's how we react to a given set of circumstances. As a dramatist you must imply why such a set of circumstances leads to a conflict. This can be projected by the behaviour of the characters, by their thoughts, their actions and how and why they think in the particular way that they do. You must explain why they are human—or, perhaps, inhuman.

CHARACTER NUMBERS

In radio drama you can have as many people in a scene as you want. Once again, the secret is in the art of illusion. There can be 500 in the crowd, cheering, or 10,000 angry workers booing their employer or their union or the government.

For practical purposes, it's best to keep the number of speaking characters small. People have a tendency to forget who's who, lose track of who said what. This sort of confusion will lead to the play falling apart. Six main characters is an optimal number. Think twice before committing yourself to a greater number. If you really feel that you need more characters, maybe add just one more. And try to make them all different, so that each one is easy to identify.

Remember, not all dramas have to involve real people. There's plenty of scope, given a wild imagination, for out-of-this-world stories. While real life is a ready source of plots and story lines to draw upon, allow your mind to range freely.

DRAMATIC CONFLICT

It is perfectly possible to make a seemingly boring set of circumstances boil with human interest. If you reach a point where your chosen subject matter or set of circumstances don't seem exciting enough, consider introducing a twist to your original concept or a fresh aspect. It all takes a little imagination — and isn't that what radio's all about?

Take, for example, a couple walking along a quiet beach on a sunny spring afternoon. They are holding hands.

Conflict? There is none immediately apparent.

Now introduce another element into this relationship. Let us suppose that the man has a large dog that he adores.

Conflict? Maybe. If his lady friend likes dogs there may be nothing more in this added element than, well, the dog. Now, suppose, the dog puts his paws on the woman's shoulders and gives her a big lick on the face. Conflict now?

If the woman still loves dogs she will probably ask the dog to get down, and that would be the end of the matter. But let us believe that she trembles whenever she sees such a monstrous beast. Perhaps she was savaged by a dog when she was a small girl, and that trauma has remained with her. Now we are approaching a conflict. There is the dog whom she doesn't like, and feels threatened by whenever she sees her lover.

Now let us suppose that she tells her friend: 'Get rid of that dog, or I go.' Now we're getting somewhere. There is now a distinct conflict, not only brought on by the dog, but also by an attempted resolution of the conflict.

Such a situation could be resolved in a couple of ways. The man could say, 'Okay, I'll send him to a dogs home tomorrow. Come around for dinner tomorrow night and he won't be here.' Such a rapid resolution would be very agreeable in real life, but in the world of drama such a rapid loss of conflict would be bad news indeed. Before we know it the couple are holding hands, and all's well between them — yawn!

So let's suppose it isn't that easy — that the man suffers an internal conflict as to whether he would rather lose his dog or his lover. The reason for this conflict does not have to be explicit. It can be suggested as somewhere distant, or merely just out of view but always lurking.

Returning to the happy couple walking along the beach holding hands; the woman announces that her son by a former marriage has just been expelled from boarding school for bad behaviour, and that from next week he will be living with them—bringing chaos into the home. Conflict? Yes—even though the boy isn't present. There is the anticipation of conflict—anticipation of what's to come for both of them.

But it's not just circumstances that bring on drama and conflict. To some extent conflict is about how individuals *perceive* their circumstances.

Suppose our male character was extremely tolerant and understanding in his outlook. Because of his temperament and personality there would be no conflict—despite the uncomfortable news about the imminent arrival of the unruly son.

Conflict can also arise when people are plunged, by fate, into unusual and disturbing situations.

A man works in a boring job in the public service, filling out forms. Not really the stuff that blockbuster movies are made from, is it? He knows his job well, and enjoys the security of the mundane existence his job allows him. He is then promoted to a job in, say, the computer area, where he can't grasp the concepts of this technology, and knows that he will be demoted, or at least reprimanded because of his apparent incompetence. Conflict? Yes, because now we have someone who is out of his familiar environment.

Again, the exact nature of this dramatic situation would depend on the personality of our character. If he were a nervous sort of person, used to being told what and how to do everything, he would feel strange in his new environment and conflict is mainly contained within the internal state of the character in his striving to cope. But if he were an outgoing type, ready to tell the section head how to run his job, the drama would be more likely to arise from external conflict.

CHARACTERS

The way people react to circumstances depends heavily on their individual makeup. In life there are strong men and weak men; strong, domineering women and those who go along with anything that's going their way. There are children who naturally fit in with any circumstances, and those who go it alone. There are the smiling, friendly people, and the grumps. There are happy people and there are moody people. This doesn't mean that you should base all your characters on real people. You will find that invented people are more obliging in a play than disguised characters from real life, because you can make them do exactly what you want them to.

If you want to write good drama, it is important to study the people in your everyday life — analyse the way they behave. How do they act? How do they react to different circumstances? Could you make them act any differently if you tried? Are they likely to say different things to different people, in different ways? Understand people, then you are ready to select your characters, and to invent new ones.

Because there are so many types of people, it should be easy to create characters to fit your situation of conflict. When you are selecting your characters, remember that they must not feel too comfortable with their lot. If they are too comfortable in their roles, the drama dies. If you find that your drama is becoming limp, the only way to breath life back into it, no matter how brilliant your plot, is to replace the character, or characters, that are bringing the play down. So radio drama is like life in that it is a combination of character, setting and action.

SETTING WITH DIALOGUE

Dialogue is the backbone of any play. The words chosen should be just the right ones for every occasion. The dialogue should convey the information in a pithy manner and keep the plot moving forward.

Take the following brief conversation:
NOOLBENGER: What time is it?
CLAXTON: Five minutes past three.
NOOLBENGER: Blast! These trains are always late.

From these few words, we can learn a considerable number of points that are (or at least should be) important to the development of the play. We now know:

- the time of day

- that Noolbenger doesn't have a watch

- that Noolbenger is impatient

- that the two characters are at a railway station

- lastly, I suppose one could facetiously believe that the railway station is on a New South Wales line.

It is particularly important to establish the setting — the place, people's dress, activities that are going on around the characters — in the listener's mind. Unlike prose, where external description, narration and internal monologue can be given free rein, the radio play must rely more heavily on dialogue for dramatic setting. This does not imply that characters have to state the obvious. For example — 'We have waited at this railway station in New South Wales for ten minutes ... it is now five minutes past three, and I think the train is late.'

Always stimulate the listener's imagination. Allow the listener to fill in the setting ... Build up a picture, bit by bit, by implication. Let the listeners do some of the work!

Consider a description of a run-down and deserted factory or warehouse. If you just have one of your characters saying, 'this is terrible, and I don't like it', you won't create much of an image, and it will do nothing to engage the listener's interest. But you could develop these same points using simple dialogue. If you had one character criticising the building and perhaps another character adding his ha'penny worth, it is possible to convey the setting in a more dynamic way. Take a real estate agent, Jones, a prospective lessee, Henry, and a mate of his, Jack:

HENRY: Looks like the paint manufacturer went out of business too, long ago.

JONES: Oh, I'm sure a new coat of paint would work wonders. Perhaps if you take a long lease, I may even suggest to the owner that he repaint the outside. It would make the place look so much nicer, I'm sure.

JACK: Yeah. I'm sure.

JONES: Oh, yes, [laughing] I see what you mean. Flakes of paint. Oh, I'm sure I could put pressure on the owner to do something about that. These premises have been vacant for quite some time, you know. I'm sure he would be pleased to oblige.

This now creates in the mind of the listener a picture of how dilapidated the building is.

Let's look at what might be inside this warehouse that we are creating. The use of a narrator to describe the setting would not be appropriate, but there is nothing wrong with, say, the real estate agent pointing out some of the features of the building, as well as reinforcing perhaps an earlier statement that he made regarding the country's economy:

JONES: Would you like to have a look around the outside first? As you can see, there is ample parking space for several vehicles. The large door gives you easy access to the work area.

[*SFX: Opening metal door*]

Of course, there's a telephone on the premises, and that is essential for any business. It will have to be reconnected. It was cut off when the previous tenants moved out. I understand they were unable to pay their bills. But of course

...

SETTING WITH SOUND EFFECTS

Alongside dialogue perhaps the most effective way of building up images in the listener's mind is by the use of sound effects. Appropriate effects can either add to features brought out in dialogue, or speak for themselves. For example, the sound of an old-fashioned cash register's bell alerts the listener to the fact that a purchase is being made. The whistle and puffing of a steam train convey the setting of a railway line or station.

If you are creating your own sound effects for your drama, you might have to experiment. Some sounds are irritating if overdone. If your drama is set on a moving train, it's fine to set the scene with the sound of the train clickity-clacking along the steel rails but imagine one hour of that noise behind the dialogue! The drama might have to be transferred into a quieter carriage. The same problem would arise with, say, a waterfall. Keep the setting near the waterfall, but just around the corner where the sound isn't so offensive. You can easily move your characters out of the noisy area:

CLARKE: C'mon, let's move out of this damn noisy valley.

SUZY: Okay. It's quieter just beyond those rocks over there.

Cutting from one scene to another is another way to give your listeners a break from monotonous and distracting background noise.

There are some activities that don't really create sounds at all, such as walking in soft sand. But this doesn't mean that such situations have to be devoid of all scene-setting sound. Think about what other sounds people might hear while they are walking along the beach. There will be the sound of the surf and the calling of sea birds. But, be careful not to overdo it, or the result might be similar to those cheap Hollywood movies where there might be one bird in the distance accompanied by the sound of a flock of angry seagulls attacking the actor!

Always remember that sounds on a recorder do not always sound like the real thing. Experiment with sound. Great sound effects can be created by the most unlikely combinations —

running a card along the teeth of a comb, or scratching in gravel might duplicate the sounds you are trying to create.

There are some good sources of realistic sound effects available if you are prepared to look for them. It is possible to buy sound effects recordings in most formats. These can take the worry out of creating appropriate sounds for your action — as long as they are played at the right volume, for the necessary duration.

Fading a sound up and down is often used to good effect for a character approaching some action. For example, if a character is running to catch a train, you could fade the sound of the train whistle up over the sound of running footsteps to indicate the approach of the train and the urgency of the situation.

A WORKED EXAMPLE—BUSINESS AS USUAL

The following excerpts from a proposed radio drama relate to three young men who are unemployed, but let us never make it so obvious in the dialogue that we have someone asking, 'Jack ... why are you out of work?' Let's be more subtle than that. From the following excerpt we soon learn that:

- the characters are at an employment office

- they are all out of work

- they have been unemployed for a long time

- there are few prospects of work for any of them in the immediate future

- Jack and Sam are careless in their personal habits and are not very bright

- Henry shows a degree of initiative and is the leader of the three.

Note how the sound effects put the main characters, Jack, Sam and Henry in an appropriate setting as we listen to their conversation. The effect of the clerk calling numbers is to create in the listener's imagination the illusion of an office; her voice need not be loud, and so it is appropriate to have her voice '*Off*' meaning 'off mic', or apparently distant from the microphone.

FEMALE VOICE: [*Off*] Number thirty-seven.

HENRY: What number are you?

SAM: Number thirty-seven.

HENRY: You'd better get up there and see what she wants then, hadn't you? Eh?

SAM: Yeah. S'pose so.

HENRY: And tidy yourself up. You'll have more chance of getting yourself a job if you look human.

FEMALE VOICE: [*Off*] Number thirty-eight.

MALE VOICE: [*Off*] And number forty-one.

SAM: [to HENRY] Yeah. S'pose.

[*Pause as SAM gets up to see the clerk*]

HENRY: I don't reckon he's even trying. He's always like that. Should take pride in himself.

JACK: Yeah. You been up?

HENRY: Yeah. I was first here today. Real keen I was.

FEMALE VOICE: [*Off*] Number thirty-three.

HENRY: Want some gum?

JACK: Yeah. Thanks.

[*SFX: Chewing gum being unwrapped and wrapper screwed up.*]

HENRY: Don't throw the damn paper behind your chair. Pick it up. Make the place look tidy. Show some respect.

JACK: Yeah.

[*SFX: Footsteps approaching, then stopping. A chair creaks.*]

HENRY: How did you go?

SAM: Same as usual.

HENRY: Want some gum?

SAM: Yeah.

[*SFX: Chewing gum being unwrapped.*]

HENRY: And don't throw the paper behind the chair. Keep the place looking respectable.

The Radio Documentary

Here, the plot does not develop further. However, this short interchange does convey an image of the characters, with their slovenly habits. And it is, after all, the characters who create the circumstances for themselves. Change the characters, and invariably you will change their circumstances. So character development in addition to plot (or action) is essential. It would be disappointing if the whole setting were provided within the first few sentences of dialogue. Develop the setting bit by bit. Drama must be carefully paced.

We don't have the resources available to a writer of prose for describing the town in which Jack, Henry and Sam live. In a book, the author can talk about the smallness of the country town, its tree-lined streets, its decline over recent times, and the demise of many of its businesses. With radio drama, it is, nevertheless, fairly easy to subtly introduce such descriptions into the dialogue as events develop. In the story of the three young unemployed men, this insight is provided by Henry's belief that there are still several real estate agents operating; Sam, correcting him, provides the listener with the details he or she needs, to build on the image already created.

HENRY: We'll go around and see a couple of the real estate fellas in town. We'll see if they've got a place we could have, real cheap.

SAM: That shouldn't take long. To see all the real estate blokes in town, I mean. There's only one left here. The other fellas went out of business. They didn't get enough customers like us.

HENRY: We'll see the one who's left then. Finish your beers and we'll get going.

All descriptions must be built up gradually in the listener's mind. See how many facts are uncovered in the next short dialogue, and the importance of sound effects.

[*SFX: Two car doors slam shut. A car is push-started.*]

SAM: I reckon the old girl needs some rings. I hope Henry buys a new one in his new managerial position.

JACK: [coughing] Port Kembla's got nothing on this old chimney stack.

[*SFX: Engine roars. Car doors slam shut. Car accelerates.*]

From this we learn that:

- one of them (Henry) has plans for a business venture
- Henry's car is old
- it won't start
- the engine is worn out, and it burns oil.

Dialogue should be made to sound human. In real conversation, people seldom keep to the point; they break off sentences, get sidetracked, come back to the main drive of their speech. Natural-sounding dialogue can mirror these interjections and side-steps, but without wasting valuable time and words. The dialogue should advance the plot in a common direction. In the next excerpt of dialogue, note how Jones breaks off his conversation and asks the three men to pull up a chair and sit down. Such events are not really important to the development of the story, but brief diversions like this add a human quality to the characters.

Returning to our play we learn about Henry's plans for a business endeavour. In the following pieces of dialogue, we gain a better insight into:

- the dubious nature of the scheme
- the doubts that Sam and Jack have for Henry's business abilities
- the nature of their business venture.

JONES: Can I help you?

HENRY: Yeah. We're looking for a cheap place.

JONES: For yourselves? To live in?

HENRY: No. To start up a repair shop.

JONES: I see. And what exactly did you have in mind? Please sit down. There's another chair behind you, sir. That's right, just pull that one up to the desk.

[*SFX: Chairs being arranged.*]

JONES: Now, what exactly were you gentlemen after?

HENRY: Oh, something cheap. Small, probably.

Interest is generated in the listener's mind as they wonder whether these three scruffies could indeed succeed in business under such difficult economic conditions.

The true nature of the main characters does not have to be revealed at the very beginning of a drama. It is better to let this unfold as the story develops. Let factual information fall into place where it feels right — and that's not always at the beginning. The following piece of dialogue could appear after fifteen or twenty minutes of action, and certainly after the main background has been developed — that is we have learned that the three young men have plans for some venture. Don't spoil a good story by parting with too much information too early in the action. Let it develop and be revealed progressively.

JONES: I see. I see. Perhaps if you could tell me a little bit more about your requirements, I might be able to help you.

HENRY: Yeah, well. We're all tradesmen, you see. And we want to open a workshop. You know, work together. That sort of thing. We reckon if we all go in together, we can cut costs.

SAM: We might all go in together, if Henry's running the show.

HENRY: Don't take any notice of me mates. They're always clowning around.

Previous conceptions about the situation in the town, the lack of work and the downturn in the local economy are reinforced, reminding the listeners of the reason for the setting up of the business and the reasons why the three of them are out of work in the first place.

JONES: I'll see just what we can do to help you — I'll just look through my listings. [*SFX: Cards being shuffled.*] You must realise, of course, that since the downturn in the economy over the past year, there are a lot more premises available than there were some time back.

HENRY: Yeah.

JONES: A lot of businesses have gone broke. Very unfortunate. Very sad. For the people, for the town, for everyone. The banks even ...

HENRY: Yeah. We're just starting out, so we'll handle things different to the way the other fellas ran their businesses. We know what we're doing.

The scene changes as the characters leave the real estate office and travel to the warehouse where Jones shows the three men the workshop. The sound effects, the car being started then accelerating, then a pause, followed by the car slowing down and stopping, let the listener know that a period of time has lapsed — one in which nothing much has happened, and certainly nothing that would have advanced the story.

SAM: We travel in style today. Wish the boss would buy something decent like this for each of us.

HENRY: Get in!

[*SFX: Car doors slam. Car motor starts, then accelerates. Hold then fade to out. Fade up engine noise, hold, then car slows down and stops.*]

A contrast in attitudes, even between different types of people, can be enhanced by a criticism of one by the other. Indeed, a contrast in characters adds interest and dramatic tension.

[*SFX: Inside moving car.*]

JACK: I couldn't be bothered doing the gardens like all these people do.

SAM: Probably they're all retired. Nothing else to do with their time.

JACK: No. Guess not.

SAM: I couldn't be bothered cutting lawns, or pulling weeds out of the ground, or ... or ... cutting the bushes, and things like that.

JACK: Naw. I guess we're all different ... I mean, us three. We've got lots to do. Probably we're more interesting than most people.

To illustrate difference and tension further, consider the following contrast in types of people — the three scruffies, and Henry's parents who are depicted here as an average, middle-class couple. Note how the sound effects add to the information available to the listener.

MR SIMPSON: It's good to see you all, lads. Come inside and have a cup of tea. Your mother's in the kitchen, Henry.

[*SFX: Footsteps on gravel. Wooden door closes. Footsteps to out.*]

SAM: No beer? He's a bit of a ...

MR SIMPSON: Well, lads, sit down. Sit down. Mum's in the kitchen making the tea for you now.

SAM: Ah. I need this rest. Been workin' real hard today.

MR SIMPSON: Huh! It's probably the change of pace that's made you tired, Sam. Well, lad, let's hear the reason for this honoured visit.

HENRY: Well Dad, we've decided that ... that is, Sam, Jack, and me ... we've decided to start up our own business. We were wondering if you could help us?

MR SIMPSON: Don't mumble so much, lad. Now speak up. I thought you said you wanted some money.

[*SFX: Teapot and cups carried on a tray.*]

MRS SIMPSON: Help yourselves to sugar and milk, lads. You'll get no servants around here.

[*SFX: Tea poured into cups. Cups rattle as they are handed around.*]

MR SIMPSON: Well, lad, out with it.

Again, contrasting attitudes add information about the characters and the plot. Consider now what Henry's mother and father think about their son:

MRS SIMPSON: Oh, I'm so glad, dear, that you have agreed to help them out. I think your generosity is going to make the world of difference to their futures. I'm so proud of our Henry. That's what I've always said about him. Deep down, he's really ambitious. He does so much want to work. The dole's not the thing for boys like Henry who have so much going for them.

MR SIMPSON: Huh!

MRS SIMPSON: Now that's not really necessary. It's a pity that you don't share the faith in our Henry and his friends that I've got.

MR SIMPSON: Huh!

HENRY: Gee, thanks Mum. Thanks.

A change of scene can be achieved in a number of ways. One is to fade out the dialogue, pause, then fade up the next piece of dialogue. Another effective way of changing scene is to have characters leaving the scene and doing something else.

MR SIMPSON: I'll get back to my roses. I've got a lot of pruning to do before the weekend's over. You will have to excuse me.

MRS SIMPSON: And I must get on with my chores around the house too. I must admit, Henry, my job is much easier now that you've found your own flat to live in.

Don't make dialogue that serves as scene changes too long, unless it develops the action further.

Attitudes can reinforce ideas. Let's listen in on a brief conversation, tinged with heavy skepticism, between Sam and Jack about Henry's plans to create work.

JACK: Have a job. By Monday morning. Create work. How do you reckon he'll create work?

SAM: Don't know. If there's no work around, we can't do the stuff. The employment mob can't find us any. The government can't create work.

JACK: Yeah. They reckon they can. For seven years the prime minister reckoned that he had been tryin' to create work. Or so he reckoned. He used to say he'd created more th'n a million jobs in that time.

SAM: Yeah. I know what you mean. Really.

JACK: Yeah. Really. Now listen ... There was half a million of us fellas out of work when he got in a few years ago. Now there's a million of us out of work. So, where's these million jobs he's created? I ask you that.

SAM: Yeah. Know what you mean.

JACK: I reckon when they create a million and two jobs, the extra two jobs might be ours. Perhaps the government can give our mate here some clues about how he should go about creating work for us, in the meantime.

HENRY: I'll do that by using my initiative. That's because you two don't have any ability of your own.

Contrasting attitudes tend to reinforce the theme of a drama. So far we have seen three scruffies trying to set up their own business. Now consider a completely contrasting outlook. In the next scene, with Henry, Sam and Jack listening in the background, the contrasting attitudes are displayed by people who are in good jobs, yet cannot be bothered with people who are less fortunate than themselves.

SHIRE PRESIDENT: Well, gentlemen, do we have any more business to discuss this evening? Rex? You would like to say something? Make it snappy, please. I'm in a hurry tonight.

COUNCILLOR COX: Thank you, Mr President. There's just one point that has been brought up during the past couple of weeks, and that is the situation regarding the unemployment problem in this town. The public seems to think we should be doing something more about it.

SHIRE PRESIDENT: Ahhr. They're always thinking we should be doing everything around here. What are we supposed to be? God? Or higher than Him? It's not our problem.

COUNCILLOR COX: There is an election coming up at the end of the year. Perhaps if we could at least look as if we were concerned ...

SHIRE PRESIDENT: Concerned! Concerned! I'm not concerned. Are you concerned, Cox?

COUNCILLOR COX: Well, no, not really.

SHIRE PRESIDENT: Is anyone here concerned? [*Pause*] See, Cox. We're not concerned.

COUNCILLOR COX: I just thought, sir, that ...

SHIRE PRESIDENT: Then don't think, Cox. Concentrate on the important issues. If those lazy bums out there helped themselves more than they do at present, there'd be no problem. No problem, Cox. Did you hear that? Anyway, it will go away.

[*SFX OFF: Mumblings.*]

SHIRE PRESIDENT: They're lazy. They don't want to work. Forget them. Let them look after themselves. Let Social Security look after them. Let the government look after them. That's why we vote for a government — to help people who can't be bothered helping themselves.

[*SFX OFF: Mumblings.*]

SHIRE PRESIDENT: Does anyone have any further business to discuss? I'm referring to important business, this time. Important business, Cox.

[*SFX OFF: Mumblings.*]

SHIRE PRESIDENT: Then let's adjourn until the thirtieth of next month. I've got a dinner engagement to go to, and I don't want to be late.

SCRIPT PRESENTATION

Now that we've looked at different aspects of script and character development, let's look at the final aspect—how to present the script for maximum readability.

On the first page of your script you should include a list of the characters. Keep character descriptions down to one or two sentences.

Business As Usual

MAIN CHARACTERS

HENRY Late twenties, scruffy appearance, panel beater by trade, unemployed.

SAM A scruffy type, mid-twenties, a glazier but has been unemployed for some time.

JACK Another scruffy type, a plumber by trade, mid-twenties, unemployed.

MINOR CHARACTERS

MR JONES A real estate agent, aged in his fifties, well educated.

MR SIMPSON Henry's father, aged in his early sixties, retired, middle class.

MRS SIMPSON Henry's mother, late fifties or so.

SHIRE PRESIDENT Well educated, arrogant man, aged in his late fifties.

COUNCILLOR COX Educated, shows compassion in his manner, aged in his forties.

The script should be set out clearly—very clearly—so that the actors can find their parts easily. The dialogue should be double spaced, with a wide left-hand margin. The characters' names should go in this margin. Specific stage directions should be included at the beginning of each scene. Most actors need directions, particularly those in community radio—only the real professionals, for example, could do without specific instructions.

The script should be typed clearly on one side of A4 paper. Use a good-quality bond paper, one that doesn't rustle as the pages of script are peeled off from the top of the pile. Rustling pages would probably not contribute much to the desired sound effects.

If you have produced your script using a computer, then alterations can be made easily.

If a piece of dialogue is ten lines long, keep all ten lines together on the one page. This will help the actors to make the dialogue flow smoothly, without hesitation.

Chapter 5 Interviewing Techniques

The purpose of interviewing someone is to elicit information. The information obtained from an interview could be for an arts program, for example, or for a short segment in a longer program, such as an interview in a news bulletin.

There are some good interviewers on radio, and there are some woeful ones. Be a good interviewer. Be professional.

When you conduct an interview, two points are worth remembering—the questions you ask, in order to obtain the information you want, must be relevant, and the answers you get must relate to your question. If the answer is not appropriate to the question, either ask the question again, or edit out that part of the interview from your program. It is your responsibility to steer the interviewee back onto the track if he or she is inclined to wander from the subject. If the answer doesn't seem clear ask yourself whether your question was clear.

Make up your mind about the line of questioning you intend to make—and stick to it. However, you may find that an interviewee brings up an interesting and relevant fact in the course of an interview that you were not aware of, or had not thought of asking—so be flexible.

Before you even contemplate interviewing someone, make sure they have the authority, or sufficient background, to speak competently on the subject you intend talking about. If, for example, you were producing an arts program about Australia Council grants to writers, it would not be a good idea to get a grant recipient to talk about the policy of the Australia Council and its funding program in general. Instead, concentrate on how he or she intends to use the grant, on the recipient's background, how the grant will further their career, and so on. Asking that person if they believe the Australian Government provided enough funding last year, or whether grants should be made available to more people, is ridiculous. Ask someone from the Australia Council who has authority to speak about government policy regarding the arts.

A good interviewer soon learns not to ask silly questions – it can result in some very sill answers. To a recent question on radio 'What was it like to work in a war-torn country?' the interviewee was polite, and explained many of the difficulties she encountered. But she could just as well have countered with something like 'lots of fun', or 'I enjoyed all the gore', or some equally cynical reply.

Ask instead something that makes sense – like 'What were some of the difficulties that you faced in your work in the [war-torn country]?' You are likely to receive a response that is more in keeping with the type of question that you wanted, and it will help the interviewee to focus on a particular angle.

Remember that your questions, and the answers given to your questions, must be clear. If the interviewee doesn't understand your question, your listeners probably won't either. And just because an interviewee understands a question, you shouldn't assume that your listeners will too. They may well lack the background knowledge that you and your interviewee have. So ask your questions just as you would like to be asked a question yourself – that is, make sure there is no doubt about what you (and hence your listeners) need to know.

PREPARATION

Prepare a list of questions in a logical order that you would like to ask the interviewee. An interview should progress in one direction only, not jump all over the place. Don't ask questions at random, and hope that from the resulting jumble of answers, you can salvage something that sounds like a well-rehearsed interview. It won't. It never will.

An informal chat, perhaps over a cup of tea or coffee, before you begin the interview is a good way to begin to relate to one another. It serves a number of worthwhile purposes:

- It will help the person to relax and feel more at ease — and when people relax, they communicate better.

- Your interviewee will often develop confidence by going through some of the planned interview points with you, knowing that what they are saying is not being recorded.

- By running through your questions, you will be given a second chance to find out if there are any that are not suitable, and also to make sure they follow on in a logical, well-developed sequence. You will be better able to do this now as you gain greater insight into the subject to be discussed.

- You will save yourself editing time later on, by dropping questions that don't produce informative answers, or were, on reflection, not relevant.

- The interviewee might suggest a good approach for the interview. If you are not as familiar with the topic as the interviewee, you could be well guided by such a suggestion. Stories, anecdotes or humorous incidents that relate well to the subject may emerge at this time, and might be suitable for including in the interview.

A good interviewer will also find out some biographical information about the interviewee, such as the person's background and interests and the work he or she has done in recent years.

You should always have read enough about the subject of your proposed interview to be able to check statements or facts with the interviewee. If you have any doubts about a statement the interviewee makes, ask him or her to explain or expand on that point. If you are wrong, you can always edit that comment out later; if you are right, the listeners will be better informed because you doubted or at least clarified something, something that was not entirely correct or clear.

INTERVIEW STYLE

Ask short questions, using short sentences, and short phrases. Avoid questions that are so long that, by the time the end of the question has been reached, the beginning of it has been forgotten.

Never ask the interviewee, 'do you think …' Of course the person is going to tell you what he or she thinks, or believes, or knows. Ask the Australia Council representative straight out, 'Is the government on the right track with its funding for the arts this year? rather than, 'Do you think the government provided sufficient money …' Ask simple, unambiguous questions. Keep multiple questions and alternative options out of your line of questioning.

Some issues are complicated. This doesn't mean that your questions need to be complicated. Nor should the interviewee's answers be complicated.

When you ask a question, allow the interviewee sufficient time to reply. If you ask a question, then surely the person has the right to respond; if the question is important enough for you to ask it, then your listeners might even want to hear what the answer is. If, by mistake, you interrupt the interviewee in the course of an answer, ask them to repeat the answer and edit out the bad parts.

Listen to answers. If a person says that the moon is blue, don't find yourself asking two questions later on if he or she believe the moon is coloured. Prevent this type of redundancy by listening to what is said — as you would in conversation with a friend.

Each question should be specific. For example, if a musician has just arrived in town from the Dominican Republic in the West Indies, don't ask the question, 'What is the Dominican Republic like?' This type of question is too general. Be specific: ask the question that relates to his or her music, or to the music or the scope for musicians in their country. Or ask about the arts in the Dominican Republic, the support that is provided to the arts, the size of audiences, and the popularity of the subject's music.

Always be prepared for answers that don't fit your preconceived ideas of what is about to be said. People see things differently. For example, if you were to ask several people to tell you what it was like to have spent the last three days on a mountain top, you could expect lots of different answers. An amateur astronomer, for example, would have found the experience exhilarating, viewing numerous faint stars through the clear mountain air. A vulcanologist on the same mountain, if it were of volcanic origins, might merely find it interesting to have spent time on an extinct volcano. You might find that a Buddhist had enjoyed a mystical experience, while a lost child might have been terrified. So ask each person narrow but relevant questions: for the astronomer, — 'Can you see many more faint stars than you can from your home-based observatory?' — to the subject who enjoyed the mystical experience — 'What was it like to meditate on the mountain top?'

ELICIT DETAILS ON AIR

A good interviewer will help the interviewee out by asking for more details or information whenever it is required, rather than leaving questions standing alone.

Suppose you are interviewing a doctor from Mali in Africa. Your interview might form a segment of a health program, and might be looking at some of the problems faced in that country. If the doctor talks about, say, guinea worm, you should persuade him or her to extend the answer, at the same time clarifying any points the doctor might have missed. Your own — even brief — reading about conditions there would have helped you decide the types of problems faced by the doctor, the residents, and the health services generally in that part of Africa. Don't forget you are obtaining the information for your listeners, not for yourself.

You may know some of the answers, but the listeners that you are serving may not know any.

So if our friendly Mali doctor mentions the guinea worm, for example, add your comment to the effect that 'the guinea worm, as I understand it, is a water-borne parasite that causes dreadful skin infestations ...' The doctor will hopefully follow this up and explain the subject more fully. But be prepared to help the interviewee. Some people have such specialised knowledge of a particular field that it is hard for them to relate to a mass audience.

A WORKED EXAMPLE

Let's consider a singing group from the Dominican Republic. You would not be able to interview the whole choir together. The microphones for a start wouldn't reach all the voices. There would probably be one or two people who would represent the group and who would be prepared to speak on behalf of the others.

Introduce the topic, then the interviewee. An interview such as this could be started along the lines of: 'We don't hear much about the culture of the Dominican Republic in the West Indies, but for the next four weeks the Dominican Republic Girls Choir will be touring Australia, performing in all major capital cities.' That introduced the choir; now for the representative: 'Ms Beatrice Singalong, the choir mistress and conductor of the Dominican Republic Girls Choir is here to tell us about the performances that her choir will give in Sydney tomorrow. Ms Singalong, you have taken the choir to seven countries so far on this tour ...'

An interview such as this, apart from the more formal introduction, could be in the form of a friendly chat, better suited to an interview on an arts topic, rather than a direct question and answer format. Talk *with* the person, rather than *to* them, just as you would when having a chat with a friend. But you will still have to direct questions to obtain information about the tour, the choir, and a whole lot more. The 'friendly chat' doesn't dispense with this aspect of any interview.

FORMAL INTERVIEWS

There are some people, though, such as councillors and politicians, where the more formal question-and-answer format is inappropriate. This does not imply that you should regard this person other than as your equal. In such an interview, you will need to take the lead. Ask the question, and if you get an appropriate answer, move on to the next question, either by continuing on from the previous answer given, or taking the interview in the desired direction.

Some people will tend to wander off in all directions, sometimes deliberately to avoid the next question they think they are going to be asked, and sometimes inadvertently because they want to talk about something that is important, or interesting to them. If the person is deliberately evasive, you might try: 'Can we get back to my earlier question regarding the funding for the tour. You said that …' For such an interview, it would be appropriate to adopt the attitude: I'll ask the questions … you answer them!'

You might be unlucky enough to interview someone who is determined to mess up the interview with a lot of nonsense. Such people might resent being interviewed, might see their time better spent doing other things, or may simply be embarrassed about a particular subject. You can't get information from someone who is not prepared to give it. On most programs on community radio, such an interview should, I feel, be terminated early, with thanks to the person for his or her time, and left at that. Only on serious current affairs programs is there room for the 'non-interview' where, say a politician deliberately avoids all the embarrassing questions. Leave such interviews to those current affairs programs. Some journalists take delight at turning evasive politicians into mincemeat—leave the job to them.

An interviewee might bring up new material that is nevertheless interesting to your program or particular interview; if time permits, you may choose to continue this new line of questioning. If it is interesting but does not fit the outline of your proposed segment, then you might suggest to the interviewee that it would make worthwhile listening on another program you are putting together, or another program by one of the other presenters. If the interviewee concurs, then continue along in that new direction. With skilful editing, the listener need not know that an interview emerged from another one, on an unrelated subject.

Interviewing a person you know well can sometimes be a problem because you are too familiar with that person — perhaps a friend or colleague. Too intimate a tone can ruin an otherwise good interview. Maintain a professional tone — the person being interviewed will usually understand that the interview is for the benefit of your listeners, not for yourself.

CLARITY IS IMPORTANT

Illustrate certain answers. If the interviewee is talking about, say, areas of land, and talks about a plot being eight hundred square metres, add for the benefit of your listeners that 'this is about the size of an average suburban block of land.' Other areas that are familiar to many people are the size of a football oval, or the length of a cricket pitch, or the size of the State of Victoria. As long as your listeners can visualise something about the same size, they will better understand the concept.

People often get confused about measurements of area. Ten metres squared is not the same as ten square metres (written as $10m^2$). Ten metres squared means an area that measures ten metres by ten metres, which equals one hundred square metres. And if you are like many people and still tend to think in terms of the Imperial system of weights and measures as well as in the metric system, be consistent. Don't talk about pounds and ounces in one question then kilograms in the next, reverting to pounds and ounces a little later. By preference use metric only.

The interviewee should be coherent, and speak clearly. Some interviews would be halved if all pauses, 'ums' and 'ers' were edited out.

You will sometimes be required to interview a person live on air – that is in the studio as you broadcast. This may be alright if you know your subject, know the interviewee to be a good speaker and are well prepared. Test your interviewee beforehand, perhaps over the telephone, to see how they perform in response to a few questions.

From time to time you may find yourself having to interview a random, unprepared person – such as when you take your microphone onto the street and ask for opinions on a particular subject. Make sure each person speaks clearly. If in such interviews you ask the same question of a number of people separately, don't include in your edited version the repeated question. Say at the beginning that you asked a number of people in a particular locality a particular question – tell the listeners what the question was – then play their responses.

There are two types of interviews that you are likely to conduct for community radio: those that will be played on air and those where you are seeking background information to compile a talk. With the latter type of interview, voice clarity is not so critical, as long as you can understand what was said during the recording.

RECORDING TECHNIQUES

For interviews going to air, recording quality control is extremely important. The studio is the best place to conduct interviews – the controlled environment and the studio equipment will ensure that you produce material of the highest possible quality.

However, you will have to record some interviews outside the studio. Be aware that the kind of portable equipment that you will use does have its shortcomings. In the studio you should have separate microphones for yourself and your interviewee, placed so that you can record the interviewee, as well as your questions. Adjust recording levels before you start, so that the interview is recorded at the correct volume. Ask the interviewee to say a sentence or two so that you can check the recording level, get his or her distance from the microphone right and play back the sample. Ensure that the equipment is recording, and that the interviewee and you stay within the range of the microphones, otherwise your voices will become too soft.

Microphones may occasionally cause an interviewee to develop stage fright. Some people see a microphone, realise that their every word and every mistake is being recorded for posterity, and clam up. In these situations a small portable recorder and microphone, placed to one side, can be less intimidating. However, recordings made in this way are seldom of broadcast quality.

Names that are hard to pronounce can cause problems. Some might simply require a little practice before you begin the interview. Occasionally you might find yourself interviewing someone who has a name that is all consonants and few, if any, vowels. Try your best; if you still have troubles with a name, introduce your interviewee and then make your first question, 'Did I get your name right?' If they have a sense of humour they won't mind correcting you.

One newsreader on an overseas radio station overcame this difficulty in pronouncing a difficult place name recently by talking about a meeting, 'wherever it was held'—not very professional.

Chapter 6 Timing

Timing in radio is important. The term 'timing' can cover two aspects of your program – choosing when your program goes to air for maximum benefit and enjoyment, and tailoring program material to fit the allocated time slot.

It would be inappropriate, for example, to broadcast a writers program between 5.30 and 6.30 in the evening. Firstly, a program other than a musical program needs concentration on the listener's part. At that time of the day, most listeners would be arriving home from work or else preparing dinner, so such a program on air at that time would not benefit many people. However, if the same program were broadcast in the mid-afternoon – with the children at school and the house quiet – listeners would be in a better position to concentrate on the spoken word and thus derive far more benefit and enjoyment. Likewise, a program of top-forty hits and rock and roll music, which would have a large following amongst teenagers and the young-twenties age group would be best suited for broadcasting in the evening and at the weekends.

Sticking a program on air and just hoping that someone listens, shouldn't be your intention. Having spent a considerable amount of time producing your program, it would be a pity if there was no one there to appreciate the fruits of your hard work. Target your audience intelligently by putting out your programs at the appropriate time.

Consider a 'typical' family – if there is such a thing – and consider the individuals in that family – those who work, those who attend school or university, and those who are employed at home. Think in terms of their work time and their leisure time.

Weekends are different from weekdays. These two days are when many people catch up with jobs that need doing around the home. It is also a time when many people enjoy listening to the radio.

Breakfast programs, not only on community radio, often seem to comprise endless (and sometimes empty) chatter about subjects of very little substance. Heavy discussions about serious subjects are generally not considered good early morning fair. Short discussions on topical issues to inform listeners about current events are fine, but do keep them short. People don't have much time to spare on weekday mornings — they just don't have the time to listen to an entire thirty-minute segment.

Identify the people who would most likely appreciate your type of program, and consider when they are most likely to be listening to the radio.

So pick your planned audience, then see if the station management can give you a particular time slot that is appropriate. Explain why you want a particular time period, and make it convincing — provide a listener profile.

Others will have the same ideas, of course, and some will want the time that you have chosen. You may have to wait a while for a particular time to become available, in which case you might have to settle for your next preferred option, with the intention of moving to the more desirable time when the opportunity arises.

A WORKED EXAMPLE

Let's look at the timing for an individual program. Say you have one hour to present 'The Environment Program'. Suppose this is a program about conservation and related issues, run on a Saturday morning between eight and nine o'clock.

Before you go into the studio, you must know how long each segment of your program will run. If it's a recorded segment, time it accurately beforehand using a stopwatch. Add up the total playing time of all the recordings you will be using in the program. They may account for, say, thirty-five minutes of program time.

If you are going to be interviewing someone live in the studio, calculate how long it should take, and be prepared to cut the person off at a particular time. Remember that some people do like to go on. Inform them in advance of the time allocated for the interview. Ten minutes would be the upper limit for an interview.

Calculate how long your script will run — read it through aloud at least twice. During this final reading, you should also pick up any howlers that shouldn't be in the script anyway. Say that it runs to eight minutes.

So far you would have thirty-five minutes for recorded interviews, ten minutes for the live interview, and eight minutes for your script: a total of fifty-three minutes.

This would leave you with less than seven minutes for music to break up the program.

You should also allow half a minute or so for your introduction and theme music at the start of the program and a closing announcement and closing theme at the end.

The starting time of your program will be 8.00 precisely. So be in the studio at least half an hour beforehand to get the interviews, music, your script and other material sorted out. Put each component into its correct order so that you can find the relevant section at a moment's notice, when you need it. That way you won't fumble during the program. Giving yourself plenty of time before the show will enable you to catch your breath and relax so that you can present your program in a professional manner.

Don't forget that the timing only runs to schedule if you do. If you cue your recorded segments so they start playing when they should, and cue your CDs so there isn't a long gap in broadcast time between them, all should be fine. If you cue a recording incorrectly, you could throw out your program by as much as fifteen seconds. Not only will your program sound less than professional, but you could very well overlap with the scheduled commencement time of the next program.

CLOCK WATCHING

Unlike many jobs where clock watching is frowned upon, watching the studio clock is essential to ensure that a program runs to schedule. A miscalculation in recording time, or interview time, can throw out a program by a significant number of minutes. Watch the clock frequently, and check that your program is on schedule. This isn't so critical in musical programs, particularly when short tunes are being played. Any small discrepancy in schedule can be adjusted for by playing a shorter track of a recording, or perhaps a longer-running tune if you have more time available than you expected.

Each minute — indeed each second — is important in programs such as radio documentaries or drama — and even classical music programs where some pieces may run for a long time. Listeners do not like to have their favourite concerto or symphony cut short because you have miscalculated the time. Watch the clock and substitute a shorter piece if you are over-running.

As the program proceeds watch the clock more regularly. By the time you reach the last quarter, every second is important.

Know the exact length of your closing theme music, start playing it so that it finishes right on time.

CHANGING OVER

Depending on the size of the radio station you are broadcasting from, and its resources, you may have to vacate the presenter's chair pretty smartly. The next program may begin from the same studio — using the same microphone or CD players and recording devices that you were using only seconds earlier. To ensure a smooth change-over, your closing theme may need to run for a little longer than it should otherwise do. You must be out of the studio and the next presenter in place and with the door closed before the next program begins. To save time in setting up recorded material or cuing CDs, you may be asked to put on the opening theme of the next program. Remember that the next program must begin at 9.00 am, not 9.03 and a few seconds (except of course if it follows on after an hourly news bulletin). But ... it's little things like this that make community radio fun and keep it exciting.

Chapter 7 Presenting

Many people involved in community radio are not interested in producing programs or in writing them, but solely in presenting them on air. The presenter is the only person usually (other than in drama and recorded interviews), that the audience gets to hear. Effective presentation extends the communicative power of written material. Presenters must know their subject. They must read or speak without faltering, and communicate with enthusiasm. Clear diction can be attained with practice.

Speaking over radio is a little different to normal speech — there must be no stammering or changing of subjects in midstream, or slurring of words, or mumbling. All words should be spoken clearly. Words should not be run together as a result of sloppy speaking: not, '... nothing happened a tall', but, 'nothing happened at all'.

Always remember that you have a duty to present your listeners with material that's worth listening to. Make it interesting to listen to. You can do it ... it's rather easy, really. The key to good radio is effective communication — the effective conveying of thoughts, ideas and information to your listeners. You must communicate with a voice that is interesting and clear, and use words that are concise and precise.

Follow the basic rules that are discussed in this chapter and you will soon be on your way to communicating effectively.

THE SPOKEN WORD

When you bring your writing to air, you should combine what you have written with a vocal delivery that makes it sound as if you are speaking, and not just reading. On air, it is all too common for presenters to sound as if they are reading — which undermines the concept of radio being the 'spoken' medium.

You can, with practice, develop a reading pattern that sounds as if you are not merely reading the copy, but communicating with your audience. Read your material through aloud a few times. Not only will you be alerted to any badly cast phrases by doing this, but you will become familiar with the material and so be able to speak faster and more confidently — just as if you were speaking to a friend. It will all flow much more smoothly. It is a good idea to try to read several words ahead of those that you are speaking. If this presents problems, read each sentence as smoothly and quickly as you are able, and pause between sentences. This is far better than faltering at every word. You will get faster, and better, with practice.

Try to develop good broadcasting habits early in your career in radio. After all, we all know how hard it is to change bad habits.

Your aim is to convince the listeners that you are talking to them — not reading to them.

When you are reading your script you will want to stress certain words or phrases. Mark these on your copy by underlining, or use a highlighter pen. Don't overdo the emphasis though. If phrases in every sentence, in every paragraph are emphasised, the overall impact will be less than the occasional, carefully chosen emphasis.

Also mark your copy where you think you should pause for effect. Mark these simply using a different mark — or colour — from that used to indicate emphasis. With only two systems of marking there is not too great a risk of confusion.

As an example, it is alright to read that the footballer had received 'a three to six month suspension ...'; but, if the pause is not in the right place — after the three — then it is easy to make this sound as though he received a '326' or a '3-2-6' month suspension. Listeners may be left wondering what a '326-month suspension' is.

Sometimes what looks alright on your written copy can sound rather strange when spoken. In a recent news report about a fire near the city of Orange (a small city to the west of Sydney), the newsreader said that the fire had been attended by an 'orange fire truck'. You would be excused for believing that fire trucks were either red or yellow. This sentence should have been recast to read, '… the fire was attended by a fire truck from the city of Orange.'

A PERSONAL TOUCH

Look through a studio window when a competent presenter is broadcasting. He or she may be reading the script, or just talking. There will not be anyone else in the studio, but often they will be making gestures with their hands and arms—just as if they were talking to another person in the studio with them. This, although it might look a little odd, will help you to achieve a more natural-sounding vocal delivery. Just be careful not to hit the microphone. A wallop on the microphone is magnified many times in the listener's ear—a degree of emphasis that isn't necessary.

Although my advice to you is to 'be human' it must be recognised that there are a number of degrees of 'humanness'. Some people regard being human, and being sloppy, as the same thing—a chance to mumble. Not at all. It's to aim for a high standard of presentation while preserving your distinctive personality in the process.

What is it that makes you enjoy talking to someone? Is it the person's relaxed manner? Or their confidence? Or perhaps a friendly tone? Or is it their total involvement in talking to you—making you feel important? It will be a combination of all these things.

RELAXED AND OPEN

As you start out in radio you will probably find it hard to relax on air, and will experience a certain amount of tension, which may well show itself as a straining of the vocal cords. But with time (hopefully only a short time) you will feel more confident and comfortable in the studio and you will be able to relax to a certain degree. Don't relax to the point where your program and presentation begin to suffer. Don't be so relaxed that you forget to cue music or make announcements on time, or forget to announce the program that follows on from yours.

A relaxed voice will make your listeners feel that you are not dictating to them—that you aren't being autocratic. But before being too friendly, take into consideration the mood of the program. Use your friendly voice whenever you can—for announcing general information, music, community events.

It might seem to you that developing a friendly voice by conscious means is rather a tall order. Perhaps you are normally a fairly reserved person. One trick is to smile as you present. Unlike on television where wearing a smile will possibly get you branded as 'The Cheshire Cat', on radio no one can see you while you are on air. Smiling will do more than just make you feel happier. The tone of your voice will be enhanced, and you will come across to your audience as a friendly person. Of course, there will be situations where a 'smiling voice' would be inappropriate—when you read out the day's funeral services, or report on a fatal road accident.

CONFIDENCE

Confidence is also essential to effective communication. If you say something, say it as though you really mean it, say it as though it has to be said, and say it as though you are the best person on hand to say it. There's nothing worse, or more likely to put off listeners than to hear a presenter stumbling at every sentence. Speak with confidence. Speak proudly! The occasional stumble is acceptable, but, whatever you say, say it well and only after you have decided what you want to say! Don't just open your microphone and talk about ... well, nothing in particular

Unfortunately, we do often hear that, don't we? Regrettably, yes, we do!.

If you're caught with insufficient material, play some music, play a promotional message announcing a forthcoming program or community event. Do anything other than say something that says ... almost nothing!

CLARITY

Do you speak clearly? You must if you are broadcasting. Clear speech is the best means to clear communication. Pronounce each and every word perfectly. Make each word stand out from every other word, separate each word without making it sound as if you are deliberately separating them. But make every effort to avoid sounding artificial or stilted in your presentation. Speak so that you can be understood — the first time.

There is an old adage about work — if it's worth doing, it's worth doing well. On radio, there should be a similar saying that if it's worth saying, it's worth saying well.

Your only tools on air for communication are your voice and your presentation — the way you use your voice. Not everyone has the perfect radio voice. But this doesn't mean that your voice is only second-rate, or that you therefore have to be second-rate in your speech and presentation.

Make the most of what you have. Some presentation and performance on community radio is superb — the way community radio should be.

A news bulletin should not be a totally solemn occasion. But it shouldn't sound as if it is a comedy session either. Use your discretion.

Be interested in what you are saying. If you lack interest in the music you are presenting, or in a forthcoming event in your community, how on earth can you expect anyone else to show any enthusiasm? Yet enthusiasm is no more than speaking with confidence and interest. Your role — indeed duty — is to make your listeners want to take part, or become involved, or become interested, or take notice of their community.

Be very wary of inadvertently saying things in the studio that you would regret going to air. When you have someone in the studio with you, watch out! If you talk to that person, perhaps during a long piece of music, or a recorded interview, make absolutely sure that your microphone is switched off. Many a sentence has been uttered on air that has been regretted. This also applies if you talk to yourself after you have cued a CD.

Several years ago on a commercial radio station there was an interview with some children — in connection with a United Nations event promoting children's welfare — where, after the presenter had spoken to the children, without realising that his microphone was still on, he ordered someone in the studio to 'get these damn kids out of here'. And many years ago a person in a country town was discussed at length on air so that all twenty thousand inhabitants of the town knew more about the person than the person knew about herself.

PACE

Pace is something that is hard to set as a standard. Some people talk quickly, others very slowly. The fast speaker would probably find difficulty in speaking slowly, and the slow speaker would have difficulties with fast speech. The only answer seems to be ... be yourself. Present at a pace you are comfortable with. This is obviously an important factor in determining how long any script will run on air.

PACE TO PRESENT YOUR PROGRAM

Consider a music program. Some presenters catering for younger people will talk at a fast rate, and will play recordings with almost no time between announcement, commercial and the start of the next piece of music. This approach will give the impression of a racy, fast lifestyle. It all contributes to speeding up the pace of life for these listeners. This fast pace would be inappropriate for a classical music program. Listening to classical music should be a more relaxing experience. The audience will probably be older as well. Use longer gaps between the end of the music and your announcement, and pause between your announcement and the beginning of the next piece of music. Quite probably your pace — the speed at which you speak — will be slower too.

MODULATION AND INFLECTION

Some people have a naturally flat voice. This does not mean that every sentence, every word, needs to be flat. Concentrate on putting at least a little modulation into your sentences, a little inflection into your words. You might be surprised at the amount of modulation that you can achieve with practice.

On radio, this is an important part of communication with your listeners. Raise the tone of your voice occasionally. Let it fall. Make it rise again as appropriate, and so on. But don't make the same mistake as a presenter I heard recently while driving through country Victoria. She modulated her voice so much — and quite unnecessarily — that it was apparent that someone may have told her just before she went on air to modulate her voice more. The whole program sounded as if she was carrying out that instruction literally. Modulate your voice within reason.

A point can be emphasised in speech by inflection of the voice. Emphasise only those words or phrases that need to be emphasised for a particular reason. Overemphasis quickly becomes ridiculous. Treat any emphasis as being equivalent to underlining words on a printed page. Not many words should be underlined, and equally not many words need special emphasis on air.

BE PREPARED!

You should have a good knowledge of the material that you are to present. If the material was prepared by someone else, ensure that you allow plenty of time to read it through aloud at least once before you read it on air; two or three read-throughs would be preferable. Make sure there are no tongue-twisters lurking there to tie you up after your microphone switch is turned on. Remember — once you have started to read it, it's too late if you encounter any poor sentence structures. If you have prepared the material yourself, it would do no harm to read it one more time before going to air.

You may know your script well. But if you plan to intersperse your words with music, don't neglect to know your music well too. Read the titles of the music or songs you intend playing. Know how to pronounce the artists' names. If you have any doubts, ask someone.

Get a feel for the program you are presenting. If there's script, recordings of interviews, and music, be aware of why you are playing the recording or the music — appreciate how each segment of your program fits in, and be aware of the relevance of each part. The boy scouts movement has a slogan that is particularly relevant to radio — be prepared.

Be prepared for unforeseen events, too. For example, equipment failure — this was pretty prevalent in the old-style community radio studios that were put together with old, disused equipment held together with tangles of wire under the console. A gap of a couple of seconds on radio seems like a minute. A pause of ten seconds feels like an eternity. It creates anxiety for the presenter, and frustration for the listener. If this happens to you, be prepared, at a second's notice, to correct the situation — either play an alternative record, or announce that the CD player isn't producing the music intended ... I'll put it in the other CD player and see what happens ...' This is where the ability to talk straight into the microphone unprepared (ad libbing) is a blessing. Some people have the ability to make an apology sound like it was scheduled — either humorously, or seriously. This is the kind of talent that can make your presentation that little bit more professional.

HUMOUR

Everyone has characteristics that are unique. Exploit them if appropriate. If you have a good, mature sense of humour, there's no harm in using it in your programs. Your audience will appreciate a program that's a bit lively. But, of course, humour must be used appropriately. Don't get the audience to laugh at the serious news items.

Determine which of your personal qualities are best suited to radio, and develop them. People trying to be funny can be a complete flop. Several years ago there were a number of serious bushfires along the south coast of Australia; many homes (and lives) were threatened. Already a number of homes had been destroyed, when one presenter on a community radio station tried to be 'funny' by playing songs that included fire in their titles – *Ring of Fire*, etc. The whole idea was a disaster. I am sure the presenter that evening, and perhaps even the station generally, would have lost a large number of listeners as a result of this pathetic performance. So, during floods in the middle of the year, don't play Slim Dusty's old record *When the Rain Tumbles Down in July*. Listeners bailing muddy waters out of their lounge rooms won't see what's so funny. It won't work as humour. That I can promise you.

Just as humour can defuse tense situations in many a social context, so too can it take the tension out of radio work – provided it is done properly and with taste.

There will be programs when you run out of time. Despite timing your program to within a few seconds, you will be unable to get through everything you intended to. Be prepared to cut your program short. Subjects like the weather lend themselves very nicely to abridgment. Instead of talking for sixty seconds about a high pressure system centred over the Bight, with another low pressure over the Tasman Sea, the latter influencing wind movements ... just say, 'the weather tomorrow is going to be fine'. After all, that's probably all that most listeners want to know anyway.

Presenting

Be alert at all times when your microphone switch is turned on. Don't daydream, or lose interest or concentration. In radio, it is the present moment, and only the present moment, that should concern you. Plan ahead, certainly, but be alert when concentration is called for.

SOUND LEVELS

Sometimes people going on air for the first time think they need to shout to be heard. This of course is incorrect. Microphones are very sensitive instruments, and if they are set up properly, there is no need to shout into them. If you talk too loudly your voice will sound strained, stilted, and forced — the opposite of what you want to achieve. Set the microphone volume so that you can speak in your normal speaking voice.

And watch those meters that indicate the level of sound being broadcast! All the sound that leaves the transmitter should be at more or less the same volume — music, recordings, and particularly your voice. It is essential that you ensure that the various volumes are maintained at the correct levels throughout your presentation.

Every piece of equipment, such as CD players and microphones, will have a VU meter so that you can check sound levels. These meters monitor the sound by measuring its average intensity. By varying the faders, or potentiometer settings, it is possible to maintain the correct balance in the strength of the sounds from the different pieces of equipment.

A mistake that many inexperienced presenters make is to adjust the volume correctly for the music or recording, but neglect to get the volume right for their microphone. Many presenters do not realise that what they are hearing when they cue music or tapes is coming through a separate amplifier. The result is that the music and the presenter's voice will be at different volumes. A satisfactory volume in the headphones during cuing is no indication that the strength of the signal going to air is correct. The only true indication is to keep an eye on those VU meters. The readings on the VU meters should be just short of the red zone. If levels reach the red zone, sound quality will begin to diminish. At the end furthest from the red zone, your listeners won't hear much at all. So keep the meters just near, but not quite, in the red.

LEARN TO CONTROL YOUR BREATHING

Another aspect of effective presenting is breath control. Don't exhale deeply into the microphone – the listeners might think you are having an asthma attack. Correct breathing begins even before your microphone is switched on. Take a deep breath and let it out slowly. This will help you to relax. Then switch on your microphone. Break up your speech with brief pauses when you are announcing so that you do not end up gasping for breath in the middle of words or sentences.

Pauses in speech can also be effective in allowing time for your listeners to appreciate what you have said. A pause that extends beyond a reasonable time can seem like an eternity. Use pauses effectively to highlight something you are saying; don't use a long pause to gather your thoughts and think about what you should have said half a minute ago.

BACKGROUND NOISE

In addition to your own presentation skills – voice, inflection, modulation, tone, pace and breathing – an important quality consideration is the elimination of unwanted studio noise. That is, all the clicks, squeaks and bangs from various bits and pieces of equipment in the studio.

If your studio chair squeaks, ensure that you are in the right position before you switch on your microphone. You should move to a minimal degree while you are on air. Get comfortable, and keep still. Thankfully, most studio chairs these days seem to be well oiled.

Then there are the clicks and bangs as cartridges and players are switched on and off. These can sound quite incidental to the presenter, but can be picked up by the microphone and the sound magnified many times over. Overcome this pollution of the airwaves by switching equipment on or off, before you switch on, and after you have switched off your microphone. If a recorded segment is coming to an end, switch your microphone on before the recording reaches the end (during the last few seconds). The music or voice on the recording should hide any interference, making for a professional presentation.

GUEST PRESENTING

Say you were asked to fill in for another presenter, maybe for a single program or perhaps for several weeks. Would you take your own program format with you? The answer is, 'Definitely not'.

Many presenters make the mistake of changing a regular format merely because they are guest presenter. Regular listeners, looking forward to a particular style of program, might well get irritated if the usual features were not broadcast when expected, or if the type of music played were different. If, for example, you are replacing a presenter for a few weeks who usually plays country and western music, then make sure that you not only continue to play country and western music, but select records that are of a similar type older tunes, or modem country and western.

Don't take along your selection of rock and roll records and think that these will do, because you like them. Remember that you are entertaining your listeners, not yourself. But having said that, it is quite alright to bring in your own personality and your own style to the program you are now presenting—as long as the type of program is not changed.

As a presenter, see it as part of the job to listen carefully to other programs and presenters and analyse what you like and dislike about them—and why.

THEME MUSIC

Theme music is important. It not only separates one program from the next, but it alerts the listeners to the fact that a particular program they want to listen to is about to begin. Some recognisable themes, say for a sports program, can have the opposite effect and are a cue for listeners to turn off the radio. Pick a particular tune for the opening, and perhaps a different type of music for the closing few moments. Pick music that people will readily identify with your program. Play the theme for a few seconds — five to ten seconds is usually plenty — and fade it down. After a brief pause, make your announcement — who you are, what your program is, and include a summary of some of the highlights of the day's program — increase the music volume to its former level and let your theme play out. Then launch into the program itself. Theme music can reflect the nature of the program — such as the theme music from the film *My Brilliant Career* as the introduction to a writers program.

At the close of the program, another regular piece of music will indicate to your listeners that the program is over for the day. Avoid cutting off or fading out the end piece anywhere but at its conclusion.

One presenter who had his program running on community radio a number of years ago had a particular closing tune that ran for say, two minutes and thirty seconds. Exactly two minutes and thirty seconds from the end of his program, the music would begin playing, even if he wasn't on schedule; the farewell and closing announcements were made while the closing music played softly in the background. This way, his programs always finished right on time — he knew the tune, and the tune 'led' him to the exact end of his allocated time.

CUEING

When cueing recorded material, make sure that the player is off air. Generally, your studio equipment will be controlled by two-way switches — 'Off' is in the middle, one way is 'On Air', and the other way is 'Cue', which means that you can hear the signal (whether recording or disc) but nothing is being broadcast to air.

Recorded interviews should preferably have an audible leader marker on them, which is not broadcast to the listeners — this is an indicator or identification mark recorded before the segment begins on the tape, such as 'The interview with Jack Horner, the local MP, recorded on 29th September begins in five seconds'. This would be followed by a five-second pause and then the recording would begin.

An amateur presenter can be caught out at any time. If a presenter plays the wrong track from a particular record, for example, the more professional presenter will let it play, then apologise (only if an apology is necessary), then play the track intended. An amateur will play half a track, take it off and mumble something like, '... I think I played the wrong one. Here's the right one, I hope'. It's reasonable to expect mistakes occasionally: some records are wrongly labelled and some have tracks that are so close together that it's easy to miscalculate the distance in from the beginning.

DYING A NATURAL DEATH
Many past programming triumphs, on both radio and television, have only run for a short time. Many popular programs have been somewhat spoilt, following the popularity of a first series, by the writers and producers trying to keep them going. Usually, second or third series are not as funny, not as tense, not as fresh as the opening programs.

The secret is knowing when to discontinue a program. As a general rule, if you are as fresh after five years as you were after your very first program, and, most importantly, your listeners still enjoy your program as much as they ever did, then there's no need to change the format. If you feel yourself getting stale then it is probably time to quit. If you have a good listening audience, then apologise to them and tell them why you are quitting — 'for the time being' perhaps. You can always resume the same format after a break of a few months.

You may avoid this staleness to some extent by sharing the program with another presenter, or even a couple of presenters, on a rotational basis. This will require you to present the program only each second or third week. You will remain fresher, and the program will stay alive for a much longer time.

Unlike times when you are acting as a guest presenter, where the format should remain unchanged, if you share a program with one or two other presenters, there is no reason why your individual styles cannot vary. You will each have different ideas, and the listeners will welcome the diversity of views, opinions and format within the program. But ... don't change the type of program, only its style.

SOME HANDY HINTS FOR BETTER PRESENTATION

Here are a few points that are worth keeping in mind.

Even the most professional presenters will make mistakes on occasions. That's only human.

An important consideration arises when you are playing an interview that you recorded, is that there will be a difference in broadcast sound quality between the recording and that from the microphone in the studio. There is likely to be a noticeable difference between your voice on the recording and your unrecorded voice. If at all possible, allow a short break between any studio preamble and your recorded introduction. Use anything appropriate (a promotional tape, three or four bars of music, for example) to separate your studio voice from your recorded voice.

Most people know which station they are listening to at any particular time. A station identification call every now and again will remind them of this. So don't announce the station identification between each record, or between each two or three records.

Presenting

During breakfast programs, many listeners depend on frequent time calls. During most other programs, frequent time calls are irritating—one time call, perhaps at the beginning or the end of the program, would be sufficient.

Time proceeds at the same rate, at all times. It is a common mistake of some presenters—even experienced presenters—to say that 'the time is fast coming up to ...' Avoid such clichés.

SPONSORS AND ADVERTISING

Community radio not only needs listeners, but it needs sponsors as well. While changes may be implemented in the future regarding advertising material that is broadcast over community radio, sponsors of programs provide some, or most, of the funding needed to keep them on air.

Fund-raising drives are another good way of gaining money, but commercial sponsorship has its place. In return, the station is obliged to return the courtesy by promoting the business, or the services that the firm offers, to the public. To put this attitude simply: treat your sponsors right—you need them! So don't run a program that a firm is sponsoring and forget to play the promotional cartridge announcing their sponsorship and business details. There are restrictions on what can be said in such announcements, but that's more a matter for the station management than the presenter.

Broadcasting time can be expensive: there are council rates on studio premises, electricity, heating, the cost of replacing recording material, CDs and other consumables. These all add up to many thousands of dollars in any one year. So every dollar you can bring into the station's funds via sponsorship of your program will make it easier for your station to keep running— and your program along with it.

FEEDBACK

To see if you are really getting across to your listeners effectively, ask someone—perhaps someone who is quite critical—if they will listen to you while you're on air, or listen to a recording of one of your programs. Ask for an unbiased opinion. Ask the person to substantiate any comments he or she makes: whether you mumble, are over-confident, or perhaps too shy and reserved. But be wise in your choice of person whom you ask for an opinion. They too may feel shy and reserved and make themselves feel better for putting down your performance. Use your discretion here. Listen to a recording of your program yourself, and judge the results critically. Ask yourself: would I like to listen to an hour or so of this program? Does it lack interest? Is the voice too flat? Too domineering? Too waffly?

From there, aim to improve on your performance the next time you're on air. Even if you think your performance was quite reasonable, try to improve, even if by only one or two percent each time. Eliminate a couple of pauses, or speak more clearly. Control your breathing better during long passages. One or two percent improvement won't seem like much, but over the course of time this will amount to a significant improvement in your on-air performance. And isn't that what you want to attain for your listeners? Of course it is. Small improvements really do add up.

Chapter 8 The Legal Aspects

The legal issues that you, as writer, presenter or producer of programs on community radio are ever likely to get involved with, will probably relate to issues of defamation, slander and abuse of copyright material.

Large commercial networks can often afford to get involved in large-scale litigation resulting from defamation or slander. Some might even welcome it because the attention those cases attract is low-cost advertising. I know that seems a strange way to look at it, but it does happen.

However, it is extremely unlikely that you, or your community radio station (which relies on public donations, subscriptions and membership payments just to survive) would be able to pay much towards any defamation settlement or the massive legal bills that usually accompany such business.

So, it's best to steer clear of saying or inferring anything that is likely, even remotely, to result in anyone taking legal action against you or your station. While uniform laws don't exist across Australia, or even between countries, this short chapter is intended to serve as a rough guide and a warning. The general — and golden — rule is that you shouldn't say anything in public that you wouldn't like to have said about yourself, or pass comments on anyone else, that you wouldn't like said about yourself.

DEFAMATION
Defamation, roughly speaking, means saying something that will tend to reduce someone's reputation, or ridicule that person, in another person's eyes. It often isn't necessary to look far to

find someone about whom it would be almost impossible to find anything nice to say. Unfortunately that person will know someone who thinks the world of him, praises his corrupt actions, his disloyalty to his community, his abuse of power, and even his abuse of his family. If you undermine such a person's public reputation on one of your programs ... watch out for that writ. It's probably already on its way to your home.

Don't undermine a person's reputation—that is, what is generally said or believed to be so about a person—and don't overrate a person's tolerance of what he or she will take from you or anyone else.

If you were interviewing a businessman who had just been extradited from Brazil with a very large suitcase full of bank notes, it would be foolish to ask him if he were corrupt. Don't even mention the word 'corrupt'. Instead, you would ask him what he knew about the five hundred thousand dollars that had gone missing from a trust account, without implying in the slightest that he had committed any act of dishonesty.

You can write something nasty about someone and delete it almost immediately. If someone reads the copy over your shoulder, that's too bad. Start saving your precious dollars for the legal case. Broadcasting your defamatory opinions is even worse.

Be alert to the dangers if you are interviewing someone who has strongly held views about some council, governmental department or commercial organisation. Be extra careful if you are interviewing such a person live. At least with a pre-recorded interview, the nasties can be edited; with live broadcasting, no such saving grace is possible.

Another constant source of worry is talk-back radio. You have very little control over what is said by a person on the other end of a telephone line. Although there is normally a time delay of several seconds between the 'live' recording and actual transmission, you must have your wits about you in weighing up on-air comments, ultimately deciding that a person should be cut off, and when. Seven seconds is not a very long time, particularly if you are quite engrossed in the conversation. A good precautionary measure is to ask listeners to phone in with their comments on a particular subject between certain times; such comments can be recorded, edited, then played on air either complete, or in an abridged form.

'But I'm only a volunteer at the station', you might plead, as they deliver the writ. Too bad. Or, 'the station didn't know I was going to say it'. Too bad. Or, 'I didn't know that the person I was interviewing live was going to say such revolting thinks about our local civic hero.' Again, too bad.

Don't use the excuse that you were merely reading from something that was already printed, and which contained defamatory material. That a newspaper or magazine was careless, or deliberately provocative, doesn't mean that you should repeat the mistake. It might be in a newspaper's (perceived) interest to publish something defamatory and then get secondary publicity from the legal case that results from the court case. The compensation and legal expenses might, in the publisher's opinion, be worth the risk because of the extra revenue that can be earned from the publicity that is bound to follow.

'But I didn't say anything nasty about him ... I said it about the organisation he belongs to ...' Such a plea would fall on deaf ears, as organisations and associations have as much right to sue for defamation as individuals. And of course, many organisations would be able to afford to spend much more money on legal representation than you, maximising their chance of a big payout.

ABUSE OF COPYRIGHT

Another legal problem arises from your use of other people's creative material. For example, if an organisation has published a booklet that is meant for internal circulation, that publication will have a limited distribution. The text will belong to the organisation or department. Every word of it is theirs. They own the copyright.

If you want to use material from such a pamphlet or booklet, as part of a program you are producing, write to the organisation that published it and ask for permission (an email these days is just fine, and so much faster than the old snail mail). Generally you will find that permission is granted freely, perhaps with a request for you to acknowledge the source of your material: 'this material was derived from a pamphlet entitled *Helping the Sick*, published by Centrelink. We appreciate the department's permission to use their material in this program.' Get such permissions in writing in case there is any disagreement at a later date as to who granted permission, and on what terms.

On programs such as those catering for the print handicapped, where a large proportion of broadcast material would be from printed copyright material (newspapers and magazines), it is that much more important to gain copyright permission and clearly acknowledge sources. Again usually an email sent to the appropriate person or organisation will suffice.

Generally, you should find little trouble in using published material in your work in radio. The original source may like to feel that its material is reaching a larger audience. In fact interest may be created in a publication that otherwise may not have been widely known.

COPYRIGHT LAWS

There are laws covering the use of printed material, and the laws are complex.

If you write an article and it is published in a magazine, as author, you retain the copyright on your material unless you sell the copyright to that magazine. So the copyright of an article may be owned by the author, or it may be owned by the publishers. But in recent years, there are further complications regarding the copyright of articles — were you asked to write the article for the magazine? In that case, the magazine might own the copyright. Copyright also applies to the publication as a whole.

So, if you plan to use text from an article on radio, approach the author or the publisher and ask for permission to use the material. If permission is granted by the author, it is courteous and sensible to write to the publisher or editor of the publication in which the article appeared and say that the author has given you permission to read the article or use it on your program ... and is that alright? Usually it will be. Get it in writing if possible, or at least make a note of the name of the person who gave you verbal permission.

MUSIC COPYRIGHT

While pirating, or copying, of recorded material such as music is not permitted, the playing of music and other recorded material over air is generally permitted by recording companies, but whether it is played with or without a royalty payment is dependent on record company policy. However, that's a problem for the station management, rather than for you to worry too much about.

Record companies, and artists, like as much publicity as they can get for their recorded material. Playing a track from a CD, and saying what it was, the name of the tune and the album, and the name of the record company, will generate more sales for the recording company. Without airplay, most people would never get to know of the existence of many recordings — sales would be dismal. And that wouldn't be good for their recording artists either.

YOUR OWN WORK IS COPYRIGHT

Protect your own work from being used without your permission by the use of the internationally recognised copyright symbol © followed by the year and your name. You may well have spent a lot of valuable time preparing a drama, or material for a documentary. Make sure you don't give someone else an easy time producing your material in their name. At the same time, make sure you don't deliberately or inadvertently 'borrow' someone else's script for use in your productions.

There are conditions covering the use of other material that is copyrighted, by provisions of the various Copyright Acts in different countries, where prior approval is not necessary, such as for fair dealings or use of material such as in book reviews or for study purposes. So if you are running a book club program or literary program, the use of short excerpts for illustration purposes should be fine without having to seek approval to do so.

If you use other people's material with permission, give due recognition of this to those writers or producers. They will want the same credits for their work as you would expect for a contribution you have made to a program.

Chapter 9 A Look at Some Programs

We have, up to now, considered how programs should go together. Let's now look at the possible content of a range of programs that you, as producer or presenter, could put to air. The following are just suggestions only, but the ideas are based on programs that have worked well in the past on community radio stations across Australia.

Seven types of program will be considered here:
1. The Music Program
2. Programs for the Print-Handicapped
3. The Ethnic Program
4. The Health Program
5. Financial Advice
6. Schools Programs
7. The Nostalgia (music) Program

This is not intended to be an exhaustive survey. To these few suggestions can be added programs covering religious views, political opinions, psychology, environmental matters, science, children's subjects, senior citizens interests and much more still. However, the selection presented below provides a good covering of the main ground.

1. THE MUSIC PROGRAM

It seems that almost the whole world enjoys music. Music plays an important role in most cultures.

There are many types of music that are popular—country and western, pop, classical, Spanish and Aboriginal or indigenous music of different countries, to name but a few. You, as a presenter, will have to decide which type of musical program you want to become involved with. You will probably already have a particular preference for a certain style of music. It is very difficult to present a program with any degree of verve when you don't have a passion for the subject material. Aim to present the music you like the most.

The overall program format will not vary much from musical style to musical style, although the style of presentation may well be different—fast and racy for pop or rock; slow and easy for classical and some slower-paced contemporary music.

Don't play a country and western tune, a Brahms lullaby and the latest Rolling Stones hit, one after the other. A few of your listeners may like a wildly varied format, but many others will not. Your listeners are precious. Keep them. All of them. If they are tuned to your community station because they want to listen to country and western music, then that's what they want to listen to. Not Brahms or the Rolling Stones. Be consistent.

Within each particular style of music, there will be plenty of scope for varying your selections. Don't just play the current hits. For example, older, seldom-heard recordings may prove very popular, particularly amongst your older listeners (see the section below about presenting the Nostalgia Program). So, as an idea for an occasional program, you could play a large portion (or even an entire program) of older records. Many listeners no longer get a chance to hear music from, say, the 1950s, and a program on community radio presenting these tunes would no doubt be popular.

THINK AUSTRALIAN, THINK YOUR COUNTRY
In which country will you be presenting your program? These days, the world is one—and through the Internet, borders and boundaries have almost disappeared. Well, for entertainment they have. Each country has its unique music, its unique musicians, and its own unique talent. In the past, for example,

A Look at Some Programs

much of Australia's home-grown culture was ignored. Yet Australia has produced many talented musicians, singers and composers. If you are presenting programs on Australian community radio, why not play Australian recordings where possible — promote Australian talent, and 'give them a go' on air.

This is not meant to imply that you should wear the grooves off Slim Dusty's albums. Even though Slim is extremely popular, perhaps other artists would be if they were given as much air time as he receives!

And the same applies if you are presenting programs in New Zealand, or any other country — play music from your own country and support your local artists. Variety makes for an interesting program, too, but vary the music only within the style you are presenting. Leave some grooves on Slim. But of course, this idea does not apply if you are in Australia and presenting a program of Spanish guitar music each week!

Every artist is an individual in this world, just like you. Some presenters frequently announce an artist as 'the one and only ...' While they may be technically correct, couldn't they say something slightly more original?

Whether you play one record at a time or four consecutively, announce beforehand what you are about to play, so that your listeners will be alerted to any favourites. It is also a good practice to back-announce those tunes that you have just played, for the benefit of listeners who caught the end of a particular tune and want to know what it was. Particularly with classical music, give full details of the recording, including the recording company, the name of the album or disc and its catalogue number.

A musical program doesn't have to consist entirely of music. You could include accompanying news and documentary items that might be of interest to your listeners; for example, you could compile a list of concerts or performances that are forthcoming in your area. You can be a source of all sorts of information that your audience might not otherwise have ready access to. Inform your listeners!

I know of a very popular program on a community radio station that consists of recordings from the 1950s interspersed with poetry readings by the presenter and his wife. If you enjoy poetry, and can read it aloud well, it might well provide an attractive, added dimension to your program. Although the scope of the music program—or any other program—is only limited by your imagination, don't overdo it. A little poetry reading is fine, but be sure to keep the amount of music and poetry (or whatever other material you include) in proportion. If it's a music program, then the content of the program should be mostly music, not mostly poetry.

Although your listeners may have music playing in the background as they go about other tasks, you shouldn't assume that they will not pick up any flaws of presentation. An audience will be fussy, even if the radio's only playing in the background.

Like any other program, musical programs should begin with a particular theme that listeners will learn to recognise. Hopefully this will encourage them to turn up the volume, and listen more attentively. Select a theme that's appropriate to your type of music—perhaps even one that has a few words in its beginning. For example, the tune that begins with the words 'May I have this dance ...' would be appropriate if your program presents ballroom dance music from the 1940s and 1950s.

The scheduling of music programs is crucial. If, say, you are presenting a program of religious music, then a broadcast time on Sunday would be most appropriate although some stations play hymns and church music late at night during the week.

For classical music, too, try to get your program scheduled on Sundays, the day of the week that many people try to dedicate to relaxation.

There may be times when you will be asked to fill in for the presenter of another program. If you are filling in, keep the program format intact. Don't change the content too much, and in particular, don't alter the musical style. Your job is to entertain the listeners, not yourself (although I sincerely hope that you

A Look at Some Programs

would be enjoying yourself at the same time as you entertain the listeners). If it's a classical music program you are asked to present in another person's absence, then keep the content classical. Don't take a unilateral decision to play country and western, rock and roll, or Zulu drum music. Remember your listeners. They are what radio is all about.

Repeated playing of the same recordings on a particular program can mean one of two things: that the presenter lacks imagination and a diverse range of taste, or that the station has a very small collection of CDs. Whatever the cause, excessive repetition must be avoided at all costs. Keep your programs interesting by presenting a diversity of recordings. Even if the studio only has a small collection of records, make sure that you play the fullest variety of tracks from those recordings that are available. You could even consider taking some of your own recordings along to the studio.

REQUEST PROGRAMS
Recently I, and a number of people I know, stopped listening to a one-hour country-and-western program that had become a request program. Over time it developed into a program where the same seven or eight listeners would request — would you believe — the same tune each week. So each Saturday morning, one knew exactly which records would be played, which track would be selected, and for whom. Deadly.

Even though you might be able to discourage the same few listeners requesting the same tune every week, a lot of people might still request one or two tunes frequently. The result is the same — either you spend a lot of valuable air time calling names and sending out cheerio calls, or you play the same tunes each week.

Play a mixture of tunes, with the more popular ones played just occasionally more so than others. That way, you should be able to please just about all your listeners each week.

Another danger of request programs is that the tunes requested may not always be available. If your personal collection, combined with the studio's record library, is extensive, it may be possible to locate and play almost any of the tracks requested. If not, you will have a lot of embarrassing apologising to do.

2. PROGRAMS FOR THE PRINT-HANDICAPPED

Statistics compiled by relevant government departments and by welfare agencies put the number of print-handicapped people in Australia at around two million people These figures are more or less consistent with those of other developed countries.

What is the definition of print-handicapped, and what are the special needs of the print-handicapped listener?

Many people think only of blind people as being print handicapped, but this is too limited a view. Anyone who does not have access to the printed word for any reason can be considered to be print-handicapped. This includes:

- people with eyesight too poor to read, but who are not necessarily blind

- recent migrants who do not have an adequate command of the English language

- people who haven't learnt to read

- patients in hospital who are immobilised

- dyslexics

- people who suffer from arthritis so badly that holding a book or a magazine, or even turning the pages, is excruciating

- those who have lost the ability to use their limbs such as quadriplegics, those who suffer diseases that affect muscles such as cerebral palsy and multiple sclerosis, and the victims of strokes.

A Look at Some Programs

In any community, there will be a proportion of people—perhaps around ten percent—who need, or who could benefit from, programs intended specifically for the print-handicapped. Other listeners who are not print-handicapped will also listen to the program if they find it interesting enough—perhaps not to benefit directly from the specific information provided, but because they enjoy some aspects of the program, such as book readings, or short plays.

The print-handicapped have some general and specific needs:

- they have difficulty in gaining access to the information normally provided by newspapers or magazines

- they are not able to read pamphlets provided by, say, Centrelink, that might outline benefits they are entitled to

- they cannot read the listings of television programs, or read the births, deaths and marriages columns in the daily newspapers

- simple instructions, such as those for operating a stove or a washing machine, are meaningless to them.

Programs intended for the print-handicapped should be designed to be as informative as possible to suit their needs. However, don't treat print-handicapped listeners as people who are different—many, of course, will enjoy the same programs as you do.

People don't like to be labelled in any way that makes them feel different. When you are announcing your program don't use terms such as 'print-handicapped'. Be more subtle and use the term 'talking newspapers', or 'readings from the morning papers'; magazine segments can be referred to as 'readings from the women's magazines'. Book readings can be called, well, 'book readings'.

Bear in mind that some programming will be of general interest, while some will be of specific interest to print-handicapped listeners. Material aimed particularly at this group could include discussions about first aid in the home in case they are confronted with an emergency; precautions they should take to prevent fires, and how to deal with them if they start. Most people cook, so your audience might appreciate topics covering food and nutrition, health and hygiene; many people enjoy their gardens, so information relating to gardens would also be appreciated. What about discussions on hobbies, or places to visit and meeting places? What is wanted for this type of program is anything that will help to make the listener's life more fulfilling.

In addition to readings from magazines or from newspaper articles, you could invite an interesting speaker into the studio to discuss, say, gardening, cooking, or some other topic. The discussion could be live to air or pre-recorded. A program will be much more entertaining if you can find an enthusiast to speak on a topic rather than someone merely reading the same material. You should find no shortage of volunteers who could provide this type of service live on air each week.

Don't forget fiction, but bear it in mind that some plays, books, short stories and serials have been heard many, many times. In the publishing industry, it is not always the best stories that are published. Indeed, there are numerous short stories and some plays that have never made it into print. Scour your own community for material that has never been performed, or read, or produced in any form before — you may be pleasantly surprised at the vast amount of written material that is available, and which would be suitable for programs for the print-handicapped as well as general arts and entertainment features. You might help to nurture local literary talent.

Make sure that any contributions you receive are indeed worth broadcasting. Be prepared to diplomatically reject those that aren't and return manuscripts with a letter of thanks. If a work has not previously been published or broadcast, then you only need the writer's permission to use it. If it has already been published, then you must approach the publisher for permission. The scope for further interesting segments on a print-handicapped program is limited only by your imagination. In addition to unpublished short stories and plays, how about serials, or 'soapies', written by local people. Also consider poetry by local poets; poems provide a welcome change from the more commonly broadcast type of material. Look around. Be adventurous. You will almost certainly find a lot of hidden material that you could use.

NEWSPAPER READINGS

Presenting two hours of newspaper readings would be an insult to the listener. It would also be extremely boring! So, if you are reading from your local newspaper, keep the items short — the first two or three paragraphs of each story would be sufficient. Short items — about two minutes at the most — are generally best received. Liven up a long segment by using two contrasting voices, say a male and a female, to read alternate items. Break up long segments with music. Do anything to prevent listener concentration from waning. Keep the program interesting. Keep the articles interesting. Amuse the listeners. Entertain them. Don't send them to sleep.

Select items that you think your particular audience would enjoy — don't read endless motions passed by your local council, or the whole sports section of a newspaper. Vary the items, their tone, and their pace. Read humorous pieces too.

Always allow plenty of time to prepare yourself before going on air. Give yourself enough time to select news items and also to read them aloud. Often what is easy to read to oneself is not always easy to read aloud. You may need to mark the copy and change sections to make them easier to read.

It is best to keep segments of newspaper readings to about ten minutes at the most. Break the segments with music. Play an episode of a serial, or some community announcements. At a reading rate of about 150 to 180 words a minute, you will get through a surprising quantity of clippings in even a ten-minute segment. Cut out plenty, and arrange the material in an order that seems appropriate. At the beginning and at the end of each magazine or newspaper reading session, acknowledge the sources of the material you use.

Avoid material that you think could be defamatory in any way.

Some material may provoke particular interest from some listeners, and they may want to follow up the article and obtain more information. It's best to repeat information such as telephone numbers, addresses, and even the names of people or organisations that they might want to contact later. So say, '... and if you would like more information about this, the telephone number is …'

3. THE ETHNIC PROGRAM

Australia today is a multicultural society, as are many other countries. There are many new Australians who, although they appreciate Australia, still feel homesick for lands they have left behind, and for their families who are now far away from them. Many also have living relatives overseas. An ethnic program has two distinct roles to play:

- to keep new citizens in touch with their family's homeland — and with what's going on there

- to facilitate the relationship between long-established Australians and New Australians—it is extremely worthwhile to provide information that helps people understand cultures with which they are not familiar.

Just about any material that relates to a particular culture could be a starting point for an ethnically orientated program. Music provides a good basis and may well attract listeners from across cultures. If, for example, you present a Spanish program, you will be catering mainly for people with Spanish roots, but with the catchy music that is characteristic of that country's culture, you could expect a lot of non-Hispanic people to listen regularly and appreciate the music you play.

What language should you broadcast in? A combination of English and the language of the culture in question works well. If you speak a foreign language in addition to English, you may wish to present the program in both languages yourself. If you are less than bilingual then you could find a co-presenter from the ethnic community in your area.

SOURCING MATERIAL

Accessing information from overseas countries can be easy, especially between Australia and countries where there is freedom to exchange information, and where the postal service and facsimile and telephone communications are good. The Internet is a wonderful resource: it's free, it's available to anyone who has an Internet connection, and to those who know how to seek out the material they need.

Remember that although you might be broadcasting in English, and have access to the huge amount of foreign material on the Internet, not all your listeners can speak English as well as their native languages. There are numerous foreign language newspapers available, particularly in newsagents in the capital cities. While a lot of migrants may buy and read these newspapers, others may not bother with them. Modern technology has made the transmission of printed material very quick and cheap. The main thing to remember with ethnic broadcasting is to steer well away from the blatant propaganda that emanates from official sources in some overseas countries. Keep information factual; don't be tempted to indulge in propaganda yourself. Leave that to the experts.

If you plan to include a news bulletin on your program, consider presenting a combination of local news and news from the relevant overseas country in the foreign language. Listeners from an ethnic background may still be finding that their command of English limits their understanding of events here. If the news from overseas is also translated into English then it becomes more widely available to listeners.

Try to identify your listeners — get some feedback. Perhaps ask listeners to telephone the studio with comments about the program. If you discover that you are catering only to people of non-English speaking backgrounds, you could tailor the program to the predominant audience and maybe discontinue the English component.

Include local information that is relevant to your listeners, such as job opportunities, training courses, or social activities in your area that might be of interest to listeners.

You may learn that a dignitary from the country you are presenting a program on is visiting your city or town. Interview people like this, as they can contribute to interesting programs.

4. THE HEALTH PROGRAM

Health issues play an increasingly important part in society today. These days, people pay more attention to their health through sensible exercise and increased knowledge of nutrition, balanced diets and healthy mind activities.

One way of furthering this evolution of interest in your local population is to present a health program, where current trends and new discoveries in medicine can be examined and discussed. This type of program can involve many specialists, from practitioners of alternative medicine to your local GP. If you live near a university you might be able to entice researchers on to your program to discuss health or medical research in their particular field.

This type of program can be made very interesting and entertaining by using a mixture of speakers, by incorporating a range of topics, and including, perhaps at the beginning of each program, the latest discoveries in the field of medicine.

The fact that you aren't a medical practitioner yourself does not preclude you from doing a splendid job in presenting a health program. Keen interest is more important. However, do not give medical advice that you are not qualified to give.

A browse through the more popular science journals will give you some good starting points — you could then get a medical expert to discuss some of these topics. Or you could ask the expert to compile a 'news in medicine' segment each week. This could then run into the main body of the program — a look at two or three of the more important issues in greater detail.

While perhaps it would be best to leave discussions of this type to specialists who have extensive medical knowledge, there is still so much you can contribute to the program, such as interviewing the speakers and writing the fillers and introductions for each segment.

5. FINANCIAL ADVICE

If you have a keen interest in finance and are able to determine what is relevant to your audience — what's important and what isn't — then you're probably the person to present a program such as this.

If you ask for advisors or experts in financial matters to assist you, make sure that they are going to offer unbiased advice and not just sell your listeners a superannuation policy. There are some 'experts' or 'advisors' who are insurance salespeople whose knowledge of financial matters is limited to selling policies. These people have only a limited place on a financial program, and, unless asked specially to talk about superannuation or some other topic, should be excluded from the more general topics. Seek people with a wider interest.

Prepare your material well, know what questions you want to ask, keep the interview on track and heading in the direction you intended, and be prepared to edit material that is not relevant to a particular program.

Give your financial programs particular themes throughout the year, such as financial advice to small businesses just before the end of the financial year, and advice after the annual budget about changes that concern small businesses. Have someone interpret any changes for your listeners if necessary.

Financial laws seem to be forever changing. New taxation laws concern almost everyone, with their depreciation allowances, the permissible deductions that taxpayers can claim, dependent and family rebates, and much more. It is not surprising that so many people are under-informed about this important aspect of their lives. Sensible discussions and informative programs about financial matters are rare – good quality programs are scarce. An interesting, well-balanced financial advice program on community radio can help put this right by informing the public correctly about what they need to know.

6. SCHOOLS PROGRAMS

Schools are more than just places where children are educated. In many areas, they form the centre of a number of important social, education and community activities.

As well as informing the community about what is happening within a particular school, such as the appointment of new teachers at the beginning of the year, the enrolment of students, such a program can also serve as a training aid in the students' Higher School Certificate media studies units, and also as a forum to display students' work. By including work created and performed by young people, you will diversify the range of entertainment that you provide. Even if the performing arts do not form part of the set curriculum for any particular year, they certainly encourage community spirit participation.

Obviously, it would not be feasible to invite an entire class of thirty students into a small studio to present a program. However, this should not prevent you from encouraging input from those school children who would like to participate.

They could arrange interviews amongst other students, or with other people who have an interest in the school and its role, for example a minister for education who might be visiting the area. Some students will want to become journalists. Let them start to develop some of the necessary skills early in their lives — while still at school. Let them interview people who have authority in making decisions that are likely to affect them in some way.

It is good to encourage students to begin thinking about which direction they might like to take after their final year. It's never too young to gain practical experience. In addition, there is increasing recognition given to this sort of extra-curricular experience later on, when students enter the job market. Such worthwhile experience will certainly give them an edge over those students who have done little outside their set curriculum.

I know of at least one school where a recording studio has been incorporated into a spare room. This not only provides facilities to allow students to put a radio program together, but is a marvellous teaching aid in other related activities, such as voice development, acting and reading. The students can hear their progress and development in these areas with the effective use of recorders and other sound equipment.

Discussion programs provide a forum in which students make known their views — their attitudes to current events, their opinions on various issues.

Aim for popularity. Make your programs as diverse as possible. With five hundred students, each with different interests, different abilities, achievements and talents, this should be easy to achieve. Some students will have a natural ability to act, taking part in plays, or will be competent readers or writers or singers or musicians. It is essential that talents should be shared as widely as possible. Don't forget the visual arts — you can display these talents through the use of words by interviewing, say, students who have entered art competitions, particularly if on a regional or State level. An interview by a student who understands the power of radio and what can be achieved by its proper use, can bring a dancer, painter or sculptor into people's lives. Encourage these students!

A suitable time to broadcast a schools program would be in the late afternoon during the week. Most classes will have finished and students will be at home – or at least free – by about 4.00 PM. That would give you the choice of five nights between about four o'clock and six o'clock. Some parents would be free to listen then too.

7. THE NOSTALGIA PROGRAM

Not all listeners to radio are young people. Many years ago, the ABC ran a request program from its Adelaide studios. That station had listeners from all over Australia, and that was before the days of the Internet. They would tune into the station, put up with the static (it was broadcast in the AM band), and just enjoy the old-style of music.

And on Saturday nights, Radio New Zealand has a request program. Most of the requests are for old music records that the broadcaster still has in its collection. I am sure many of your own listeners might appreciate a program of music from a former era – the 1940s to, say, the 1970s. And that's where there might be a challenge. All music recorded in those days was recorded on old vinyl records – the thirty-three and a third records, or even the seventy-eights (referring to the rotational speed of the discs). Another challenge might be – does your station have an old turntable to play such recordings? Do you have the means to re-record the music in a format that can be played over your community station? Software is readily available for computers to make possible transfer of sounds from turntables (particularly modern ones build for just this purpose) and the sounds can then be converted into a digital format. While you are playing the old style of music appreciated by so many listeners, you are making the process so much easier for yourself by playing it using the latest facilities. Did I mention copyright? While it is not legal to copy recordings, there should be few problems if they are transferred into another format and played over the radio, as long as the new copies are not used beyond the studio, or given to other people. But be careful!

But assuming you have a turntable, and have not been able to convert the sounds to CDs or tapes, the process of playing them, and cueing the records, is so different to what's required for CDs and solid-state recordings.

PLAYING OLD LPs

Old records tend to collect scratches. If these are deep enough, they will cause the needle to jump forward to the next groove, or back to a previous groove—repeatedly. This is called backtracking. Always listen to the music that is playing so that you can intervene quickly if there are any problems such as backtracking. If backtracking occurs, turn down the volume control, carefully move the needle one or two tracks further on and return the volume to its former level. If the problem continues more than a couple of times, apologise to your listeners and take that record off the turntable—even mark the record jacket so that neither you, nor any of the other presenters, are tempted to play it again. If the record is popular, suggest to the station management that a replacement copy be sought—if one can still be found, or one re-recorded on to a CD.

Another problem sometimes encountered with records is whirring. This is caused by a record turning at an irregular speed, sometimes caused by warping. There's nothing you can do to fix this problem immediately, but placing a weight carefully on the record overnight might cure the defect. Before replaying the disc on air, play it privately—if there are still problems, put the record into the 'never to be played again' pile, as such problems are a waste of air time and lead to a lot of frustration for the presenters.

Cue records with the switch in the 'Cue' position. Put the needle at the beginning of the record, and turn the record slowly by hand until you hear the first sound (other than record crackle and static); turn the record back a quarter to one-half of a revolution. Turntables take a short while to build up to the correct speed. If the needle were to be placed right on the beginning of a track when you started it up, the first couple of bars would sound terrible as the turntable picks up speed.

But if one of your old vinyl records is likely to backtrack (that is, jumps back on itself and plays one or two tracks repeatedly), take this into consideration.

Over the past few years LP records have progressively been replaced by compact discs, or CDs. Record companies have stopped making vinyl records and even cassette tapes, replacing them with CDs as the main media for music. While there are numerous records still in existence, CDs have a number of advantages over LPs. The sound quality of these discs is superb; the players are very easy to cue (it's mostly a matter of selecting a track and pressing the button at the right time—the track starts playing almost instantly; the range of music available on compact disc is increasing rapidly, with much of the music previously released on vinyl recordings being re-released on CD.

TO CONCLUDE

This chapter should have given you some ideas about how to present a diversity of programs on your community radio station. I have suggested some of the ways to approach particular programs that should appeal to a wide range of listeners.

Remember it is your program that you are presenting on community radio. You should include whatever material you think is relevant to your interests, and the interests of others.

You could create programs for other interest groups and organisations that are under-represented in the media. These could be programs to inform, stimulate or bring together people with similar views on life—such as writers, environmentalists, conservationists or even those with political interests.

The interests of any group can be furthered by being more widely known within the community. Organisations can gain support (and respect) from the public through voicing their views in a logical, well-presented way. Public sympathy can be broadened towards a particular issue by publicity and explanation. Not only can radio bring together people of a particular persuasion and inform them of the latest issues affecting them, but it can also enlighten them about the issues and concerns of other groups within their community.

There is, of course, a far greater range of programs that are possible than the few outlined here. Get involved in your community and create programs to inform people and share information with them. Remember that skills not used are skills that become lost; talents not used are talents not shared. People want programs that are different from what's available on the mainstream stations.

GETTING INVOLVED

It is easy to become involved in community radio. Locate your nearest community radio station (check the Internet. If in Australia, a good starting point is the website of the Community Broadcasting Association of Australia at www.cbaa.org.au). If there is more than one community radio station in your area, pick the one that you feel could offer you the best scope for your interests, and approach the station. Tell the staff there that you want to become involved with presenting a program, or writing material for others. Make yourself known to those already preparing and presenting programs that interest you. Help them out for a while, see how it's done, who does what, and find your own niche, or create a new one when air time becomes available.

All community radio stations run training courses for those interested in presenting programs. Take part in one of these to find out what the different knobs and dials on the console are for, how the equipment works, and why it works the way it does.

If you fear that not enough people would be interested in your ideas, then think again. Unless your ideas are extraordinary, you can be quite sure that there are others who will want to listen to and share what you have to say to be informed, educated or amused.

Community radio is your radio station. Use it, and enjoy it. Let others enjoy it too through your participation. Community radio really is fun, and it's exciting too. Now that you are better prepared for your experience on air, take that deep breath, turn your microphone switch on, and ... You're On Air!

Chapter 10 Broadcast Technology

About thirty years ago, I became involved with a community radio station that relied on equipment that was vastly different from what one would find in a studio now.

Most, if not all, the equipment was scrounged from commercial radio stations. Those stations would ring our manager and tell him about a pile of discarded equipment they were throwing out, with the instructions to come and take what you want, the rest will go to the tip. So we did. And from that discarded equipment, and using twisted-wire technology, our community radio station was built.

Did we have computers? What were they? That's right—they were those huge machines that were housed in a specially constructed room, with their own air conditioning unit, to keep the equipment at its correct operating temperature, seldom varying by more than a degree or two from its preferred temperature.

Today, even the smallest community radio studio will, at least to some extent, be controlled by the use of a small computer.

And in those days thirty years ago, there were two turntables in the studio to play vinyl records—one on each side of the console, and no CD players. Today, thirty years on, some studios still have turntables, but they are not considered part of the normal equipment. They have been replaced by CD players that give incredibly clear sound, based on digital output—no scratches, no whirring, no sounds other than the sounds recorded onto the CD themselves. What a difference CDs have made.

But even now, there are other devices for storing recorded music and sounds. They are like the memory cards in your camera, or flash drives you use in your computer. They can store an incredible number of tracks of music, radio plays, poetry readings — anything your audience will want to hear. The presenter plugs the device — memory card or flash drive — into the computer, where they can select the track to play, and it goes to air without any clicks and bangs in the background.

Computers in the studio have become very cheap, easy to use, and very reliable — the qualities that small community radio stations will be using as their measure when selecting equipment for their studio.

Many people have become famous for their accurate predictions of future trends. There are others, however, who have made predictions that didn't quite turn out right. For example, it was predicted in America that the motor car would have very little general appeal. The head of a leading computer company predicted back in the 1970s that the demand for personal computers would remain small, and they wouldn't be worth worrying about. No doubt someone saw the telephone as of limited value and felt sure that such a novelty just wouldn't take off.

In the 1930s, the Federal Communications Commission (FCC) in America saw little merit in FM (frequency modulated) radio, and delayed issuing a licence so that tests could be carried out to judge the viability of this type of broadcasting technology. The FCC, too, had made a poor judgement, for FM radio is still here many decades later, and has proven to be ideal for radio transmissions, particularly for transmission into local areas.

Although FM generally has a shorter range than AM broadcast signals, this is offset by improved quality of reception — crystal clear and virtually free from most types of interference, including thunderstorms. It's almost like listening to a compact disc playing in your lounge room. Stations broadcasting on the FM frequency can also broadcast in stereo.

Broadcast Technology

As the technology used in radio receivers improves, so must the technology of broadcasting improve to satisfy the listeners' expectations. Listeners now demand the best radio reception, and broadcasting stations must ensure that their transmissions are of the highest possible standard in technical quality to match that demand.

DIGITAL VERSUS ANALOGUE

In analogue audio, signal information can be amplified satisfactory up to a certain point. Beyond that point, however, distortion and noise are increasingly added to the signal. This impedes comfortable and enjoyable listening at higher volumes. In addition, variations in play-back occur — the speed of the tape for example — and each source of distortion is added to the next.

Digital audio broadcasting takes a completely different approach to the handling and storage of signals. Digital technology involved breaking down the sound into data 'bits' which are reconstructed by the reverse electronic process, into sound. The signal is carried as a series of zeros and ones. In theory, the numbers are carried throughout the system without information loss — therefore noise and distortion are eliminated.

With digital sound editing equipment, station promotions, sponsorship messages, as well as all other audio editing functions can be done simply and quickly. The same controls that are on conventional analogue equipment are used. Standard faders adjust the monitoring levels of each track. On-screen menus provide easy access to editing functions, such as cut and copy, and digitally stored sound effects. If an operator is confused at any stage, he or she simply touches a help button to find out the next step, or presses an 'undo' button which wipes the editing for a fresh start.

Thirty years ago, we broadcast in the AM band of the radio spectrum. It was right on the edge of the bandwidth, and many radios were not able to tune in to that frequency — it was simply off the dial.

But the common form of transmission is in the FM band. This band came into Australian broadcasting during the 1970s and has revolutionised broadcast transmission.

AM band picks up static from outside interference, such a thunderstorms, electric hand tools being used in the garage, and even the neighbour's electric cake mixer in the kitchen. FM band is not subject to such interference.

Many stations transmit in both the AM and FM bands, while other newer stations are able to broadcast only in the FM band.

The AM signals carry a long way, they can be bounced off the upper layers of the atmosphere, and then be picked up a couple of thousand kilometres way, often in other countries. This is the advantage of short wave signals.

With digital audio broadcasting (DAB), the signal is transmitted as a series of digital impulses. There is no interference whatsoever. However, there may be some limitations with DAB as there are with transmissions in the FM band, and relates to distance.

One country can broadcast its programs, and often propaganda, right around the world.

And the future of broadcasting? The BBC and other radio stations in England, Europe and parts of Asia are transmitting in digital audio broadcasting technology. Australia has started to broadcast in digital radio, which is considered to be the next generation of radio broadcasting technology.

At the time of writing, the ABC is broadcasting in digital radio in some of the main capital cities, with plans underway for the future extension of services to other capital cities and regional areas. Digital radio will not be replacing current services, whether those be AM or FM broadcasting. It simply provides another choice in how we will be able to enjoy our radio.

Digital studio broadcasting extends all the advantages of digital audio equipment and will give a sound of about the same quality as that from a compact disc. DAB transmits in the very high frequency (VHF) band.

Microphones used thirty years ago were big and cumbersome, and not very visually appealing. Now, they are compact, can be concealed so the person you are interviewing does not become struck with fright when they see the microphone recording their every word they utter.

Some microphones can be angled so they pick up sounds from only one direction, others used for recording dramas, where the whole sounds of the studio are needed for the right effects.

Other microphones are suitable for a wide range of recording, such as recording whole choirs or orchestras. Others are available with background noise rejection, where anything other than the voice being recorded directly into them is not picked up. Other types, suitable for talkback radio segments, or where the presenter is taking telephone calls on air, can have headphones incorporated with the microphone as a single unit.

STUDIO CONTROLS

Many presenters from the old school will be familiar with a console that was controlled by an array of large round knobs. The round knobs on earlier consoles have largely been replaced on modern studio equipment by sliding faders. These faders perform the same functions as the traditional knobs and volume controls, but are operated by a small sliding action. These are easy to use, the presenter can see at a glance which faders are in use, and those that are not, and the relative degree of one to the other, such as the level of music playing under the voice of the presenter.

THE RISE OF THE CD

Long playing records, or LPs, belong to a past era, although their content is still appreciated by many listeners, hence the popularity of many nostalgia musical programs. Music is now released on CDs plus, increasingly, mini discs. CDs have even replaced the cassette tapes. Many old recordings have, over the years, been transferred on to CDs, their sound improved with distortions and crackles removed, and are now released in stereo. Some CD players available for broadcast use can store several hundred CDs, and these players can be linked, expanding their potential storage capacity to several thousand CDs, each of which can be played at random, or in a predetermined order. Information is displayed clearly on the computer monitor for the benefit of the presenter — the track number, name of any CD, the time remaining on a particular track or the time elapsed since the start of a particular track.

The cue button allows the presenter to preview the beginning of the next track to be played while another track is still on air.

Is it too much like science fiction to expect a group of community radio stations to call on one central storage unit of CDs, with each station accessing tracks from the thousands of CDs in the communal resource? Perhaps not.

COMPUTER CONTROL IN THE STUDIO

Today's radio automation systems use computers that control any number of playback devices such as recording machines, cartridge players, CDs, and even turn on microphones. A station can be run without moment-by-moment, hands-on control.

The heart of the system is a computer. It can control large numbers of events, which an operator enters from a keyboard. These might include fader instructions, inserts and special effects. These can be mixed or merged. The display on the console tells the presenter what is happening, and what is about to happen.

With some computers used in broadcasting, all operations are carried out using a touch screen display in the studio. There might be a mock-up of the console, with start/stop buttons and fader switches. The information on the computer screen includes record details, fade-end details (whether the music ends abruptly or fades out), the length of the fade, the artists performing, and much more. All the information is held in a database on the hard drive of the computer. The computer can include all sponsorship

130

announcements, forthcoming events, or the system can be run on automatic, playing predetermined selections of music one after another. Nevertheless, any information can be called up as it is wanted. It is always there, ready to be used.

A typical broadcast studio computer will wait for the presenter to tell it what to do next, such as run a series of announcements, or play music. The presenter can cross fade using programmable cross-fade timers which can be pre-set, such as two or four second fades.

Technology used in broadcasting, as it is anywhere, is constantly changing and pushing ahead. If you are involved with community radio, you must be prepared to learn to use the new technology available, or be left far behind. Having the latest equipment in the studio is one thing, but it is only as good as the people operating it. Some, or all, of the equipment in the modern studio may at first seem rather daunting and confusing, and it may take some presenters some time to become familiar with it.

Community radio should have the best possible equipment consistent with the station's available budget. Much of the equipment used in the modern studio has come down significantly in price in the last fifteen or twenty years. Computers that used to cost twenty-six thousand dollars cost no more than a couple of thousand dollars, probably a lot less.

There are numerous grants available these days, mainly through the Australian Government, and various State governments. Some of these are applicable to community organisations such as community broadcasting studios. The money, if the applicant is successful in securing a grant, can be used to buy equipment for the good of the community the station is serving, or to buy equipment to make the lives of the volunteers easier, which hopefully has the benefit of attracting even more volunteers.

And with better equipment, even if it is purchased through monies received from grants, makes any community radio station more attractive to volunteers, and in turn those volunteers can provide a better service to the community they serve. But like all new electronic technologies, prices decrease exponentially over time. Just look at how the prices of computers, colour television sets, and mobile telephones have decreased at the same time as their performance has increased. At the time of the writing of the first edition of this book, digital audio radios cost over $1700. Now, a local supermarket chain has them on special for $28.

Twenty years ago, a recording was made, generally with a cumbersome tape recorder, and the writer or typist had to type out the interview. Now, with voice recognition technology coming with any small and inexpensive recording devices, the recorded interview is put into a computer, and the words processed and edited as if they were normal script.

I live on the south coast of New South Wales, but I listen to many programs coming from the studios of Radio New Zealand, more than two thousand kilometres away.

I don't even use a radio any more — short wave reception has deteriorated so much I can no longer pick up the programs on my radio. Instead, I get the clearest sounds possible through the Internet on my computer. And recently I started learning French. I listen to a variety of stations that are in France, but broadcasting over the Internet. One could think the studio is only next door, as the sound is incredibly clear. The same applies to so many broadcast stations around the world. They are using the Internet to broadcast their programs further afield than was ever thought possible only a few years ago.

A check of the website of the Community Broadcasting Association of Australia (www.cbaa.org.au) shows that many community broadcasting stations too are connected to their audiences through the Internet, sometimes expanding their range of 'broadcast' to several hundreds, or even thousands, of kilometres.

Is it possible, then, for you, as an individual, to run your own radio station? Yes, it is, for there is a lot of equipment available for just this purpose — the small, home-based broadcast studio that would be useful to particular groups and organisations, such as bands, and environmental groups, and perhaps political parties. By broadcasting over the Internet, these studios are not subject to the rigid licensing requirements of those broadcasting over the airwaves.

Even though community radio tends to follow behind commercial broadcasting, with the introduction of newer technology, everyone involved in community radio today should expect to see changes continue to be introduced in their studio.

This chapter can only, at best, provide a brief insight into what is in use in some of the newer and more advanced broadcast studios today. Newer equipment will no doubt be introduced into community radio stations across Australia. What was considered a luxury in studios of fifteen or twenty years ago are now considered essential to do a good job in broadcasting to local audiences.

Chapter 11 Community Broadcasting Codes Of Practice

All community radio stations in Australia are governed by codes of practice. If you are a volunteer, familiarise yourself with the codes. If you are elected to the station's board, then certainly familiarise yourself with the code.

The codes are there to safeguard you as a volunteer, to safeguard your community radio station, and to give to the community that your station serves, what it needs in the way of broadcasting.

You can download the Australian Community Broadcasting Codes of Practice from the Community Broadcasting Association of Australia, at their website www.cbaa.org.au. No doubt if you are involved with community radio in any other country, then most countries will have similar codes for you and the radio station to follow.

The complete codes of practice are a rather extensive document. But don't be alarmed. It's there to tell you, and tell your station, how best to deliver programs for your listeners. Because volunteers are vital to the success of any community radio station and its programming, you, as a volunteer, are covered by the codes of practice.

They also help you if you have a run-in with other volunteers, and with the management of the station. All complaints will be addressed (perhaps to a lesser extent if a complaint is of a trivial time-wasting significance).

Because of the differences between mainstream broadcasting, as in commercial radio stations, and community radio, the scope for vastly different types of programs on community radio are possible, indeed encouraged by various broadcasting acts that cover community broadcasting.

Because Australia is such a vast country, geographic and cultural differences are to be expected. So community radio can fill a role in regions throughout the country by aiming at smaller populations of listeners. Community radio stations in Australia are expected to respect the standards of the community they broadcast to, and are expected to respond to user needs, and broadcast what the audience wants.

Because community radio stations cater for such a diverse range of interests, just about everyone can have a say on community radio. There are cultural stations, sporting stations, and radio stations catering for the print handicapped, ethnic groups, Indigenous groups — especially their different cultures. The guidelines are there to remove prejudices based on ethnicity, race, language, gender, sexual preferences, physical or mental ability, occupation, religion, cultural and political beliefs.

Because community radio can play such an important role in reflecting the Australian character, the codes of practice ensure that all groups are well represented.

This basically means that if you want to present a program on a subject, then you are well within your rights to do so, as long as the material is in good taste. This means do not advocated the use of non-prescribed drugs, or drugs for social use, or to suggest behaviours such as suicide, including advice about this topic. It also means you don't set up your program to merely criticise a religious or cultural group. If you don't see eye to eye with some groups, always remember that those members probably don't see eye to eye with your views either. They have a right to be heard, just as you do without being criticised or laughed at all the time.

The codes of practice cover the broadcasting of music too. Always play at least a quarter of Australian music. The only exception to this is if you are presenting an ethnic program, where the Australian music content can be reduced to ten percent of Australian music.

Operating standards are important, as we would naturally expect. We don't want to listen to endless rubbish, presented in the most sloppy manner imaginable, do we? So you should be getting a good idea of why the codes of practice are so important in community radio.

If you deliberately breach the main rules of community broadcasting, then remember that broadcasting licences are not a permanent feature. They can be revoked, the conditions amended, and so on. So keep your programs in good taste, and to a high standard.

Other aspects the codes expect of you to promote peace and harmony in your community. Australia has been a multicultural country for several decades. Respect that. If you can't, then turn your talents to another use.

You are also expected to pursue the principles of democracy, access and equity. This is especially important for minority groups who are under-represented in the media.

You are also expected to enhance the diversity of programming choices. This is good, because it gives you a motivation to try something new, something different, and something perhaps out of the ordinary.

As a volunteer on a community radio station, or involved with its day-to-day management, you should ensure that the news and current affairs, documentaries and feature programs, including interviews, provide access to views not adequately represented by other broadcasting stations in your region. You should present only factual material, make sure it is accurate, and make sure you correct as soon as possible any mistakes you make. And make sure you always present your news, or your viewpoints, without trying to mislead your listeners, editing out content that will sway the listeners' beliefs one way that was not intended by the interviewee, and don't withhold relevant material that would complete the full picture for your listeners, rather than only one side — your side of the story.

Because community broadcast stations are not supported by paid advertising, the stations, and the programs, are not dictated to by large corporations that dictate only the content they want on the program they sponsor. Indeed, under the code of practice, stations are allowed to play five minutes of sponsorship (as distinct from blatant advertising) each hour. The sponsorship is not allowed to reflect the nature of the program. A sponsor's announcement about his or her business could come before the local news broadcast, before a drama, poetry reading, book readings, or anywhere else during the day.

Community broadcasting stations must be independent. That means independent of political parties, independent of big business, and independent of all other matters that influence commercial broadcasters.

Community radio stations in Australia are expected to support and develop local arts, and local music. This is good, as it gives local artists a chance to be heard. After all, if a local artist's recordings were never played on the radio, how would anyone know of their existence? They wouldn't.

Community radio broadcast stations are expected to provide a service for the community, and should not make a profit from the community. Although all radio stations have fundraising days, and extended broadcasting times of some programs to raise money, that money is used to buy new studio equipment, to update old and failing CD players, and to buy a new computer that will only enhance the quality and performance of your next program.

If you have a particularly bad day on radio, or if your station management sees fit to go its own way and breach the codes of practice, there are mechanisms to bring you, and particularly your station, back into line. All complaints must be investigated by the Australian Communications and Media Authority. What action the organisation takes is, to a large degree, dependent on the severity of the complaint made. Remember that the ACMA takes its duties seriously. But ... if you always do the right thing, don't stir up hatred in your community, and if your station does the right thing by you, the volunteer, and by the audience it serves, then no one need fear anything. Most stations broadcast for years, indeed decades, without any complaints being sent to the ACMA.

Each community radio station would have on the premises a document that outlines the standards of training offered to all volunteers, and also detailed financial arrangements so the station remains viable at all times without getting into serious financial trouble.

The community is changing all the time. And so the intention is to update the codes of practice from time to time to reflect the changing community.

Appendix

A Sample Script Written For Radio
Soils and Dust

Farming methods threaten the soils they depend on. Even soil fertility is threatened by agricultural practices. Yet soils are the basis of our very existence; without food, without agriculture, we don't eat. If land is overstocked, soils are abused, and every last bit of goodness is extracted from them. Then, when we can't do anything with them, they are abandoned. This problem is becoming increasingly urgent as human populations increase.

On the earth right now, we have all the soil we are going to have in our lifetime. It can take a thousand years or more for soils to form to a sufficient depth to be useable. This makes soil one of our most precious resources. But I believe it's also one of the world's most abused resources, for which we have yet to find a satisfactory substitute.

Let's consider what soils are, and let's look at their demise.

Soils are not composed of just one or two ingredients. They are complex materials; each type of soil possesses different physical and chemical properties, and comprises a combination of many parts: elements, ions, minerals, organic matter, oxygen and other gases, water and inorganic material. Every cubic millimetre of fertile soil contains millions of bacteria, fungi, worms, micro-organisms, and other invertebrates. Soils are a mixture of all these things and more.

Because of their incredible biological activity, I would suggest that soils could almost be considered to be alive. But with intervention, it's easy to kill them, to render them sterile, unsupportive of plants, and unproductive for agriculture. That's the easy part. The difficulty is breathing life back into them.

Agricultural soils must contain sufficient moisture to combat periods of dry weather that can occur at any time of the year, and for any duration. When reserves are low, the growing season for plants, such as grasses or pastures, will be short, with insufficient feed available for livestock.

Effective water control is possible by taking proper care of the soil, maintaining a reasonable vegetation cover at all times, and ensuring a good reserve of humus.

During the next hundred years the United Nations reckons that the world's population will have increased from the present seven billion people to possibly around fifteen billion. And, if the Australian Bureau of Statistics calculations, based on present rates of increase in population, prove to be correct, Australia's population could rise from the present twenty-two million to well over forty million people in the same time. The people then will have to depend on the soil that is remaining. By the end of this century, there may not be much of the existing soils left.

Australia has been practising agriculture for just over two hundred years—in many parts of the country, it has been for only one hundred years or less, yet there has generally been a marked deterioration in soil structure, and fertility, and in the volume of soil remaining. The cost of replacing the minerals lost by the removal of the top few millimetres could well be in excess of one hundred dollars per hectare. The cost of nutrients lost from very fertile soils could well be ten times that amount. The loss of even a small amount of topsoil reflects heavily on the operating costs of farming.

A farm, neglected, with the soil blown away, or washed away year after year, will have a short life. Yet we have less soil in the world than we had one hundred years ago, less soil to feed an extra eight billion people in the next hundred years. The topsoil lost worldwide is now estimated by scientists at twenty-five billion tonnes every year. Much of the cause of this soil depletion is drought, and wind, and poor farming practices spanning several farming generations. But the problem gets worse—not better. And many of these problems can begin with salt—that white menace that causes loss of soil structure, and loss of vegetation cover that would normally hold the soil together.

Look at the dust storms that blow across continents. Australia has frequent storms that dim the sunlight. America has them. Other lands have severe storms that carry fertile soil and deposit it in the oceans. A dust storm can carry upwards of a million tonnes of topsoil—a million tonnes of fine, fertile soil. A million tonnes of fertile topsoil lost in an hour would have grown thousands of tonnes of feed for tens of thousands of animals, and feed for the people. That topsoil lost during a one-hour dust storm represents tens of thousands of tonnes in equivalent fertilisers worth perhaps millions of dollars—the cost to replace only the minerals lost. A quick loss indeed, and very expensive.

NASA's satellite photographs of the earth show huge dust storms almost on a daily basis—millions of tonnes of soil dust blown across China, or across the Atlantic where the soil removed is not deposited back on to the ground, but lost in the oceans. Some dust storms have been so intense that visibility is reduced to a few metres. They can turn daylight into darkness.

Dust storms can change the atmosphere to yellow, or red, depending on the source of the dust—or, more correctly, the soil. Which country did it all come from? It could have been from just about anywhere, from any continent.

Loss of soil and soil fertility by erosion is not confined to lands in distant places. It occurs wherever soil is disturbed for agriculture. Losses from areas in the Darling Downs in south-eastern Queensland are estimated at up to one hundred tonnes per hectare—every year. The soils there may be deep, but I wonder how indefinitely can losses of this magnitude be sustained, and production maintained, at present rates of soil depletion?

The El Nino is often blamed for causing the droughts, but El Nino doesn't cause the dust storms and the significant loss of soils. Blame inappropriate farming practices. Blame salinity that results from inappropriate farming practices. Blame deforestation. Blame overgrazing. Overgrazing during a severe drought results in loss of soils ... salinity ... deforestation. But if you must blame something, you need to look further than El Nino.

Many people show a distinct reluctance to benefit from the lessons that should have been learned from the past. We've learned nothing from the desertification around the world estimated by some scientists to have increased by two and a half times during the last century alone. We've learned nothing from the dust storms that are becoming more frequent. We look at the thick clouds of dust over the continents and show no remorse, not appreciating that the cause of those dust storms is invariably our abuse of agricultural lands. Obviously, by our disregard and lack of remorse for those clouds of red dust, it seems that we don't know what's causing the problem. Perhaps we just don't care.

The time will come when we must take action to overcome our abuse of the land that feeds the world's population. But those who are well fed, with fresh meat on their tables, and meat in the refrigerator for their next meal, should not overlook the fact that the world is facing difficulties in feeding all the people on the planet. It feeds the wealthy, but many countries are struggling to adequately feed even a small fraction of their populations—even disregarding political situations in various parts of the world that exacerbate the problems of hunger. Perhaps Australia is lucky to feed its own population. With land that is constantly being eroded and worn out, how much longer can we support ourselves? And what of those people of other countries who are less well off?

At the height of a dust storm in Victoria during the early 1980s, the dust extended across the entire width of Victoria, and stretched many kilometres from North to South. The yellow cloud was over 300 metres deep when it struck Melbourne, but in other areas it extended thousands of metres into the atmosphere. Scientists estimated that about 50,000 tonnes of topsoil were stripped from the Mallee in western Victoria, with approximately 1,000 tonnes of it being dumped on the city of Melbourne, leaving the ground bare, and exacerbating the effects of the drought. On that single day in 1983, 50,000 tonnes of fertile soil was removed from Victoria's agricultural system. And that was in only one day.

The New Zealand Alps on the South Island are often turned red, or brown, because of the loss of Australia's topsoils that are blown across the Tasman.

Desertification around the world is not something that happened once, way back in history, and should now be forgotten. Our agricultural practices have increased the extent of deserts in the world from a little over one billion hectares in the early 1900s to more than two and a half times that area in about 100 years. That's one and a half billion hectares taken out of the world's farming system, yet the world's population increased significantly during the same period. The deserts are increasing in size, because we are making them increase.

It's a waste of time to plough sandy, infertile soils, to have the little that remains blow away in the first storm. It's pointless to develop hillsides where one torrential downpour will — forever — remove the topsoil. It is a waste of time to develop pastures in those parts of a country where rainfall is inadequate to grow grasses. What last year might have been a ploughed field can, after heavy rains, consist of a series of deep erosion gullies. These are not productive; their loss to the farmer is appreciable; the inconvenience to the farmer is significant, and the cost to the country, enormous.

What can start off as a small gutter a few millimetres deep will, over only a few years, become a gigantic gully; square metres of erosion become square kilometres of erosion before very long. One square kilometre of land that has reached that final stage may not seem like much. Sometimes that area will total all the land on a farmer's property. It happens that way.

Frequently. It will remain only as a reminder of the better times that could have been won from that land, had the soil been treated with the respect that is essential if food production is to be maintained.

A thousand properties that have reached this stage of degradation add up to millions of dollars in lost profits and lost production, and hundreds of thousands of hectares of previously fertile agricultural land removed from production. The eroded land is abandoned. We look for somewhere else to initiate the same processes we used to destroy our previously farmed land.

A lack of vegetation allows winds to blow away much of the finer soil particles; wind carries them high into the air for considerable distances. As I said before, silt and dust from Australia is frequently observed in quantity in New Zealand. Soil blown by winds from the western portion of Australia can be observed far out over the ocean. Once the finer soil particles have been removed, what remains will be the hard clays, an impervious pan that will resist further wind erosion but this will be of little value to both present and future agriculture.

Wind erosion can be severe when fields are ploughed. Yet it is common to see dense clouds of soil blowing away behind a tractor, each year slowly but surely reducing the available soil. On cultivated land with little impedance to the flow of water, the rate of soil removal will be high. Down slopes, water erosion can be quite significant even over relatively short distances, and over short periods of time. Water can be concentrated into definite, well-defined channels with a still greater force with which to remove still more soil. Loose soil is easily broken down further, with particles being carried in suspension.

Yet, even a thirty percent cover of shrubs or trees, particularly in dry regions, is sufficient to greatly impede wind movement close to the ground. Substantial vegetation cover may be the only feasible method of preventing the initiation and continuation of the erosion processes. But ... where are the trees?

Appendix

Established trees seldom have a smooth surface under them. Trees drop leaves, small branches and litter on to the ground, which impede the flow of water so that it moves very slowly beneath them. Hence, the removal of soil particles is reduced. But ... where are the trees?

Salinity is an ever-increasing problem around the world. It is the rendering of large areas of once productive land barren so that no vegetation, no pastures, can grow there. The removal of trees often initiates soil salinity by raising the water table. Salt builds up in the soil due to inappropriate farming practices.

While the area of land affected in this way is large, the loss of productivity is serious. Losses caused by salinity result in economic losses of millions of dollars annually; that lost through other salinity problems such as seepage, even more.

The carrying capacity of much of the pastoral lands in Australia now is less than it was a century ago, despite the many millions of dollars that have been spent on efforts to improve productivity. The more we remove from the soil and the more we alter the soil's structure, then the more work we will have to do to breath life back into our soils. Only then will our soils again produce enough food for all of our people and all of our animals in sufficient quantities.

But that will take time, it will take energy, and it will take money.

Do you have the time to plant trees? Do you have the energy to organise information and events to spread knowledge of our soils widely in the Australian community? Do you have access to the ways government funds are allocated; for instance do you know anyone in government who you can influence to help to save our soils?

Index

Index

Index

Index